The Crisis of Creativity

The Crisis
of Creativity

GEORGE J. SEIDEL

UNIVERSITY OF NOTRE DAME PRESS
Notre Dame—London

Preface

The Greek word κρίσις from which our English word "crisis" derives is, like so many words in Greek, many-faceted in the variety of its meanings. It means a "separating," a "picking out of the good and the bad"; it is thereby also a "turning point." A crisis is a time of difficulty in which one must make a decision, and that decision can result only in a change of direction. It represents a turning point.

The crisis whose nature and historical roots we shall attempt to lay bare in the pages that follow is also many-faceted. But in the complex interconnection of these various factors Western civilization is faced with a problem of no small consequence.

Thus, in order to lay bare the complex character of this crisis, I shall attempt to trace it back to its roots. And these roots, I am convinced, are largely philosophical (as will be seen from the chapter dealing with Francis Bacon) or at least can best be interpreted by philosophy. And since these roots lie deeply buried in the historical ground of our Western culture, laying them bare will necessarily involve a great many historical digressions.

These historical digressions are not taken and followed for their own sakes, but rather to appreciate better the character and history behind the crisis. This is, I believe, the fundamental reason why man studies history. He desires to understand why he is the way he is, or why the world he

v

lives in got to be the way it is. Therefore, it is entirely typical of man to become concerned about the history that is his in a time of crisis. He naturally begins to wonder about his philosophical and historical ancestors when he begins to suspect that one of them may be behind his present difficulties. He becomes concerned about his past, the ideas and movements which influence his present, especially when some of those ideas—handed down and accepted from generation to generation as true and certain—and the institutions created by those ideas begin to break down or wear thin under the stress and strain of new problems, new crises. Then does man find it necessary to reflect upon those ideas, trace them back to their sources, attempt to appreciate them in their influence upon his life and, finally, to determine whether they must be called up for review, criticized, changed, or even rejected. This critical review of history is critical for man's own history.

In this process of laying bare the historical origins of the phenomenon we have chosen to call the crisis of creativity, many of the elements in the character of creative work will also be brought to light. Nevertheless, this is not yet another book on "how to become creative" or "how we, too, can spend creatively the greater amount of leisure time which has been offered by automation in business and industry." In this study I have in no way attempted to lay down some magic method whereby the reader may become creative. If creativity is something individual and personal, as I shall argue that it is, then general rules as to how absolutely everyone may become creative are out of the question. Not all people could be, or even would be, interested in becoming creative.

Neither have I attempted here to study and analyze the autobiographical statements made by creative artists, scien-

tists, and inventors, who may have left some record of how
they came upon their new ideas. Most probably the creative
person knows as little about his creative gift as does anyone.
In fact, many artists tend to regard their creativity as something of a "mystery," the wellsprings of which ought not
really be analyzed, lest an overly self-conscious analysis of
their creative gifts might cause the springs to dry up.

Whether this feeling is universal or true is beside the
point. What seems to be the case is that creative people, in
their productive years, are less concerned with analyzing
their creative gifts than with actually using them. Possibly
they are simply too busy and too involved in the actual work
of creating to take the time to stand off from their work and
view their "gift" and its operation from afar.

And this is what the analysis of their creativity would involve, namely, a critical standing off, abstracting themselves
from their personal involvement in their work. Once this
was done, one of the elements necessary for creative work,
namely, personal involvement, would no longer be present.
And without this element being included in the analysis, it
is difficult to see how the artist's analysis of his work would
be of much assistance. Indeed, after the years of productivity have drawn to a close, the creative person may attempt
to reflect upon his gift; but since that element of personal
involvement in actual creative work is no longer present,
such descriptions often prove cold and overly analytical.

The approach which I have adopted, then, is historical
and philosophical. It is historical in its attempt to lay bare
the root factors involved in the crisis of creativity, and thus
in the nature of creativity itself. It is philosophical in that
it deals fundamentally with man, with his modes of knowing, and thus also with the way that he deals with his world
—more specifically the creative way he deals with it. With

this aim in mind, it should be clear that many of the thinkers who have discussed creativity or the various aspects
which may throw light upon its operation are not studied
primarily in and for themselves, but rather to elucidate and
clarify the many-faceted crisis of creativity and the nature
of creativity itself. This is not, then, a historical study but,
rather, the attempt to learn from history, using that which
is learned as a springboard for my own thoughts on the
question.

It may be objected that I have taken something which is
essentially simple and have rendered it hopelessly complex.
This is possibly true. However, this is also one of the ways
that philosophy works. Philosophy, it has been observed,
complicates the simple in order to simplify the complex.
Creativity, at least for the creative person, is something
essentially simple. He does it naturally and effortlessly. It
is, as we say, "second nature" to him. Nevertheless, human
life, of which that creativity is only a part, is something
far from simple. Hence in complicating something which
is essentially simple, we may better be able to simplify the
complex thing that is human existence. As Alexander Pope
observed, not without a certain justice, "The proper study
of Mankind is Man."

For a great deal that follows I am indebted to Dr. William
Dickerson, O.S.B., with whom I had the pleasure of con-
ducting a seminar on "Creativity" in the spring of 1964, to
Bruno Laverdiere, O.S.B., artist-in-residence, and to the
many teachers, students, and friends with whom I have
discussed many of these ideas. In other words, many of these
ideas have been "stolen" from others, even though those
from whom they were "kidnapped" might have difficulty in
recognizing their very much changed offspring. I would also

like to thank Mrs. Vincent Hayward for her careful typing
of the manuscript, Adrian Parcher, O.S.B., for his careful
reading of the manuscript and for his many valuable suggestions toward greater clarity of expression.

G. J. S.

Contents

Genie ist zwar nicht Sache der Willkür aber doch der Freiheit, wie Witz, Liebe und Glauben, die einst Künste und Wissenschaften werden müssen. Man soll von jedermann Genie fordern, aber ohne es zu erwarten. Ein Kantianer würde dies den kategorischen Imperativ der Genialität nennen.

Friedrich von Schlegel, KRITISCHE SCHRIFTEN

1

Introduction

In 1900 the first and in 1901 the second volumes of Edmund Husserl's *Logical Investigations* were published in Germany, and within the next fifty years phenomenology saw itself well established as the predominant philosophical movement on the Continent. Within this phenomenological tradition of descriptive analysis, and yet striking out boldly beyond it, Martin Heidegger in 1927 published his *Being and Time* in the journal edited by Husserl.

Two of the most influential works in what has come to be the Anglo-American tradition of philosophy, with its strong emphasis upon logic and the logical analysis of language, were undoubtedly the *Principia Mathematica* of Bertrand Russell and A. N. Whitehead, the first edition of which appeared in 1913, and Ludwig Wittgenstein's *Tractatus Logico-Philosophicus*, written during World War I and first published in 1918. With these two works, and the teaching of Wittgenstein at Oxford, the traditions of mathematical logic and language analysis received their strong impetus in English-speaking countries.

In the area of literature James Joyce wrote his *Ulysses* between the years 1914 and 1921, and finally had it published in 1922. With this work the "stream of consciousness" technique was established in modern literature. In the same year T. S. Eliot published *The Waste Land*. This poem, along with his other works, introduced a pessimistic and despairing picture of the world into modern English poetry. In 1926 Ernest Hemingway published *The Sun Also Rises*, and in 1929 *Farewell to Arms*; and with these and many other works the stylistic influence of Hemingway began to exert its effect upon writers, not only in English but in other languages as well.

In physics many of the original ideas that have dominated man's understanding of and increasingly great control over the physical universe were developed within the first quarter of this century. *Planck's Constant*, appearing in 1901, set the stage for the new physics. Albert Einstein's *Special Theory of Relativity* was published in 1905; his *General Theory*, in 1916. Ernest Rutherford's work on radioactivity, as well as his and Niels Bohr's picture of the structure of the atom, represented work done in the early part of the twentieth century. Finally, the extremely important theory of *Quantum Mechanics* developed by Werner Heisenberg dates from 1925, his *Uncertainty Principle* from 1927.

New movements were taking place in music during the same period. Igor Stravinsky had presented his brilliantly orchestrated ballets *Firebird* (1910), *Petrouchka* (1911), and *The Rite of Spring* (1913), opening up wide new possibilities in the exploitation of rhythm and instrumentation for composers to study and use. At about the same time the influential twelve-tone technique of Arnold Schönberg came to the fore in Vienna. The "twelve-tone roll" first made its appearance in an oratorio fragment in 1914 and was quickly passed on to Schönberg's disciples. This technique of radical atonality has become one of the major forces in modern music. Written in this tradition was the powerful opera *Wozzeck* by Alban Berg, a student of Schönberg, which was produced in Berlin in 1925.

If we note carefully the dates of these major masterpieces in the arts, the artistic and scientific breakthroughs of the twentieth century, we will immediately discover their tendency to localize themselves within the first thirty years of the century. In fact, it would appear that the basic techniques—the fundamentally new ideas which have dominated the intellectual, artistic, and scientific areas of our culture in the twentieth century—were born and nourished largely within the years 1900-1925, and that we, the beneficiaries of these new discoveries and developments, have been living off the original ideas of a previous age. It is true that many new products and inventions have been developed in more recent years, such as atomic energy, the Laser beam, television, and so forth, to mention only a few; however, these and others are less fundamentally new and original ideas than they are the technical elaboration and implementation of the ideas of theoretical physicists working in the early part of this century. And the same might be said of the more recent developments in the arts and humanities, for example, that they represent a working out of ideas and techniques based upon methods and theories developed earlier in the century.

The key to all things human is time. And particularly in the area of the arts some critics are quick to point out that it takes time for society to judge the worth of a work of art, be it literature or whatever. They say that there are most certainly works of talent and originality being produced at the present time and that it takes time to determine whether a particular new style, method, or technique will become profoundly influential, provide new challenges, open up other possibilities, and bear rich new fruit. In other words, it takes time for a new method, technique, or style to be developed, and it requires still more time to judge its lasting value and influence.

In order to explain the apparent dearth of fundamentally new and creative ideas in the theoretical parts of various sciences, some scientists point to another problem involving time. The vast and complex new experimental instruments and equipment that scientists have at their disposal have provided a plethora of new experimental data and observations which requires a great amount of time simply to study, let alone to formulate into a new synthetic picture of the physical universe. Similarly, scientists point out that they have a tendency to adjust their experiments to the large and expensive machines they have at their disposal, which tends to complicate rather than simplify the task of sifting the already vast stock of information that must be taken into account in any formulation of new ideas and theories.

The same problem of time occurs in the arts, and the humanities as well, as a result of what has been termed the "knowledge explosion." In the area of philosophy, for example, there has been no lack of new publications in recent years; in fact, the quantity might lead one to believe that a philosophical renaissance of broad proportions is in the offing. The number of new works in literature and criticism is no less staggering. Librarians complain that they are being deluged. The explosion of knowledge does not necessarily imply an explosion of creativity. In fact, upon careful examination many of the so-called new works in the area of the humanities are often either historical studies on other writers and thinkers—some indeed exhibiting profound historical insight—or copious anthologies and uncreative textbooks, the market for which seems inexhaustible.

The very amount of time required to come to terms with the veritable explosion of knowledge and information may, indeed, be one of the more immediate causes for the lack of truly new and creatively original ideas. For the very time required to cope with the continued and continuing expansion of knowledge in all directions may reach a point of diminishing returns that can approach the absolute zero of mental paralysis, even of intellectual despair. In architecture, for example, the new techniques and materials available make the formation of a "contemporary style" very difficult. Many architects admit that the rich resources of steel and concrete construction have barely been tapped.

Again the key is time. When there is simply not enough time to take into account all that could or even should be taken into account, and when one is overwhelmed by the more and more complex character and demands of society upon one's time and energy, it is difficult to get out from among the trees to comprehend the forest. Only careful and mature reflection can bring man out into the open, and this again requires time—time that is not always at one's disposal, given the many and conflicting demands of an ever more complex society. In such a situation the potentially creative person may find himself given over to a vast number of insignificant details, so that the task of finding the time and energy required to work his way out of the forest of fact may appear impossible.

In view of this there are those who have suggested that the blame for the lack of creatively original ideas must be laid at the doorstep of society itself. They insist that it is society that either provides or fails to provide the proper atmosphere in which creativity may take place. And this, in their opinion, society has failed to do. And here again the element of time may be said to enter. For it may indeed be that society does not wish to foster the creative new ideas that might usher in yet another new age. We live in an age of rapid, even violent, change. Possibly the rate of change is even now too fast for society. Time is required for men to absorb the already vast changes experienced within the last several decades. In other words, if it is true that society provides or fails to provide an atmosphere for creativity, then there must be very good reasons why society does not desire the creative new ideas that in other respects it so desperately needs.

By the same token, in a world that "shrinks" daily in size, as ever more rapid and efficient means of transportation and media of communication become available, events tend to happen more "quickly." The age is a hectic one, not because time is somehow speeding up, but because the complexity of the world is expanding in inverse proportion as it is shrinking in size. It expands in complexity and shrinks in size through the more and more efficient and comprehensive media of transportation and communication, causing events to become known more quickly throughout the world. This only increases and makes more complex the information that must be taken into account. It also means that more and more time must be devoted to the lives and destinies of other peoples throughout the world as we become less and less separated from them by distance and time. And this simply increases the complexity of the world in which we live, a complexity that takes more and more time to know and interpret.

With the ever growing complexification of society, with persons and peoples being drawn ever more closely together, there is another phenomenon that easily tends to occur, namely, a certain "leveling process"—a process, if it does not actually render creativity more difficult, is bound to change its character. In other words, when a society demands equal rights—or at least equal opportunity—for all its citizens, it is only one step further to the incorrect conclusion that everybody be like everybody else. It is the subtle fallacy of "normality" often parading under democratic guise. Not that this "normality" is ever clearly defined. It is seldom, if ever, spelled out in clear and concise terms. It can only be designated negatively. Those who may deviate from the inexactly defined mean of normality are segregated. This can be accomplished in certain cases by the courts, with the help of psychiatrists. However, even then it is done on the basis of what society has decided, but never spelled out, as "normality."

In other cases it is the educators who determine normality. Thus the bright young child is removed from association with his less gifted playmates, segregated into special schools and put into accelerated programs, so that advanced instruction, generally in the specialized areas of science and mathematics, may be given. This is done so that society may be assured of a supply of bright young technicians and scientists. It may even be admitted that the children thus segregated are not really given an opportunity to develop "normally" in association with their own age group; but this admittedly "undemocratic" program is justified by social and political necessity. Brilliant young minds are needed, and more of them. This particular "natural resource" must be fully exploited.

Such educational "crash programs" are made necessary by the general leveling process that has taken place in education as a whole. It is for this reason that brilliant young minds must be given special accelerated programs. And yet, as we shall attempt to show, this very segregation necessarily involves a one-sided development of personality which will, more than likely, fail to foster what it was designed to produce, namely, the truly creative thinkers required in the arts and sciences. For it is indeed questionable whether the overemphasis in one particular area of study to the neglect of other areas or to the neglect of the social and personal side of the individual can produce those truly creative minds that are required.

The key to all things human is time. This is no less true of human inventiveness and originality, one of man's highest potentialities. Creativity requires time to grow, to mature, and to flower. And on this score society has the pleasant duty of allowing this delicate offspring to grow and develop fully within itself. That is why with the increased complexification of society, with the accelerated time at which events happen, and with the veritable explosion of knowledge and information in all areas, patterns of creativity are changing as well. Both society and the creative individuals within that society must be alive to these changes.

In the past creativity was largely an individual affair. But with mankind being drawn ever more closely together, and with the resulting complexification of society, creativity will also tend to become more "social." Thus many recent discoveries in science and industry are more and more the result of "team effort." This is becoming true even in the humanities.

Nevertheless, such a change in the pattern of creativity does not obviate human effort. Genuine creativity will always involve individual reflection. This is the ultimate human instrument or "tool" of creative work in no matter what area, and no matter how many reflective minds may be involved. And it must be the training and development of this indispensable "tool" (this *organon*, which in Greek means "tool") with which both the creative individual and society as well must be concerned. It is this tool which Aristotle, Descartes, and Bacon attempted to study and analyze so carefully; and it is for this reason that we turn next to these thinkers and the way they attempted to understand and develop this ultimate human instrument.

2

Methods of Discovery

The ultimate organon or tool of discovery is the human mind. But the question is whether that tool is apt and fit to perform the functions demanded of it without some sort of prior training and development. In his *Metaphysics* Aristotle criticizes those who come to special studies in philosophy without any prior training in logic. As he says, they discuss the terms upon which truth should be accepted when these should have already been settled in the study of logic or "analytics."[1] What is this necessary discipline of analytics, and what is its purpose and function in the thought of Aristotle?

THE ORGANON OF ARISTOTLE

The science or art of analytics does not appear in Aristotle's division and classification of the sciences. It is neither a theoretical knowledge whose end is truth, nor is it a practical knowledge whose end is action.[2] Nevertheless, the fact that logic is not given a place in his classification of the sciences does not mean that Aristotle considers it unimportant. On the contrary, he considers the analysis of the processes

11

of human reasoning as the absolutely necessary preparation for the study of philosophy, in the same way that Plato considered mathematics as a necessary propaedeutic for philosophy. In the pedagogical order, in any case, logic for Aristotle is "first philosophy."

It was, one may suppose, in keeping with this place of logic in Aristotle's philosophical scheme of things that the word organon (instrument or tool) came to be applied to the logical works of the Aristotelian corpus; though, as we shall see, the application of this term to his logical works can be and was, in fact, misunderstood. For although it is true that "analytics" constitutes for Aristotle a necessary preparation for doing philosophy, this does not mean that he in any way considered it an organon or tool in the sense of a necessary method whereby truth or new discoveries were to be attained. This is particularly the case if we take the word "method" in the rigorous sense that it has gained since the time of Descartes. In other words, whatever Aristotle's organon might be, it is not a philosophical method in the Cartesian sense of the word method.

The primary task which Aristotle set for himself in his logical works was the analysis of the syllogism.

> If all men are mortal,
> And Socrates is a man,
> Then, Socrates is mortal.

However, it soon becomes apparent that the syllogism is not of itself designed to lead to new truth or to new discoveries; in fact, it necessarily presupposes such new discoveries. Indeed, in order for the laws of syllogistic reasoning to be formulated, both thinking and discovery must have already taken place. Hence, far from providing an organon or tool for discovery, far from presenting some startling new method for finding new truths, Aristotle's analysis of the laws of syllogistic reasoning simply studies the way men actually do think, if they think consistently and logically. And this implies that something must already have been thought—meaning that an element of discovery must already have preceded this thought.

In other words, before it is possible to reason to the conclusion that Socrates is mortal from the more general principle that all men are mortal, even when this is accepted with the provisional "if," we must determine or discover that Socrates is a man. An element of discovery is already implied in any formulation of a syllogism. Thus even though Aristotle would insist that it is only possible to know *scientifically* by demonstration—it is the syllogism, he says, which is productive of scientific knowledge[3]—still, any knowledge given by means of argument must proceed from pre-existent knowledge.[4] We shall return to this shortly when we discuss Aristotle's notion of "induction." The point we must make here is that knowledge is produced by means other than the syllogism. As Aristotle says, induction also produces knowledge.[5] Thus even the scientific knowledge established through the demonstrative syllogism must rest upon some pre-existent knowledge.

Thus when Aristotle characterizes logic as an indispensable tool of philosophy, he is not implying that prior to his formulation of syllogistic reasoning there was no one who thought logically—any more than he would say that, after the rules of the syllogism had been formulated, this was the only way in which new knowledge might henceforth be gained, even though he might insist that scientific knowledge could only be *demonstrated* in terms of syllogistic formulation.

But even though the syllogism does not represent some sort of magic method for gaining new truth, for Aristotle it is nevertheless not unproductive. As we suggested above, even if no new truth were gained through the syllogism, it is necessarily implied even for any formulation in terms of syllogism. An example from Aristotle may best serve to illustrate this.

If it is true that B can be said of C, and if A can be said of B, then (οὖν)A can be said of C. Thus if C represents "planets," B, "nontwinkling," and A, "proximity," then if nontwinkling can be said to be a property of planets and if proximity can be predicated of that which is nontwinkling, then proximity can be predicated of planets. According to Aristotle this is called a syllogism of "fact."[6]

There is a variation of this which Aristotle calls the syllogism of "reasoned fact," that is, a demonstration through causes.[7] This consists in reasoning that if proximity or nearness can be predicated of planets, and if nontwinkling is an attribute of proximity, then it is *for this reason* (or by this cause) that planets do not twinkle. The proximate cause of the reasoned fact, says Aristotle, is the middle term (proximity or nearness). Proximity as an attribute or property of planets had been gained, it may be recalled, through the syllogism of fact, which had reached the conclusion that proximity is to be predicated of planets through the proximate cause of yet another middle term, namely, nontwinkling. And this "middle term" was gained, as Aristotle insists, from sense perception or induction.

And here we encounter the creative elements necessarily involved in syllogistic formulation. There is the element of sense perception or induction. There is the uniting and synthesizing factor of the middle term.

By the middle term Aristotle means that which is ". . . itself contained in another and contains another in itself: . . . if all A is predicated of all B, and B of all C, A must be

predicated of all C."[8] There must be a middle term found
in both premises of all figures.[9] And this middle term must
be connected with the minor, and the major with the middle.[10] Only in this way can the necessary connection, which
is the conclusion, in any way be known: whether it be a
conclusion of "fact" or one of "reasoned fact." This element
of necessary connection, so important for any demonstrative
knowledge, must be obtained through the middle term.[11]

This, then, is one of the creative elements in what might
be called Aristotle's organon of discovery. It consists in "seeing" the middle term. For in forming a link of syllogistic
reasoning, whether of fact or of reasoned fact, it is necessary
to see the connective links between one premise or proposition and the next one. Even in order to juxtapose these two
particular premises side by side, so that they might lead to
a conclusion of whatever sort, there must be a point where
they connect and a reason for their necessary connection.
And this necessary relating must be "seen."[12]

Or as Aristotle puts it in the same passage, the man who
is expert at seeing the middle terms most quickly, the one
most practiced in the art of seeing connections, the one who
sees the major and minor terms most clearly and grasps the
middle terms *as causes*, is the man with a "quick wit"
($\dot{\alpha}\gamma\chi\iota\nu o\acute{\iota}\alpha$).[13] The choice of this particular Greek word is, I
think, significant. It is made up of two words: $\overset{\prime}{\alpha}\gamma\chi\iota$, which
means "near" or "close by," and $\nu o\hat{\upsilon}\varsigma$, which means "mind."
The mind "close by" is the mind that is right at the juncture
of the middle term with the major and minor. Such a mind
"sees" quickly the connection between the major and the
minor term. It is right there. And the object of any inquiry,
as Aristotle insists, always consists in finding this necessary,
connecting middle.[14]

However, there is an element of discovery even prior to

the logical formulation achieved through the quick-witted joining of two premises through the middle term. For, as Aristotle insists, we learn by induction as well as by demonstration. Demonstration is from universals; induction, from particulars. But since universals are only gained via induction,[15] then this means that for Aristotle all knowledge is achieved by means of induction. This derivation of knowledge via sense perception and induction could already be seen in the syllogism of fact noted above, in which the conclusion was reached through the necessary connection of the middle term "nontwinkling." This middle term, as Aristotle says, was the proximate cause of the conclusion, but was gained by means of sense perception or induction.

Hence, even behind the quick-witted "seeing" of the relevance of the two middle terms in their connection with a possible conclusion, there must already have occurred the element of discovery in the actual process of induction.

What does Aristotle mean by induction? The Greek word ἐπαγωγή means, literally, "to take in," or "to bring something in" (hence, the Latin-rooted translation "in-duction"). But how are these primary or immediate premises containing the all-important connective middles apprehended or induced? First of all, they are not innate, says Aristotle, nor are they gained from higher states of knowledge; rather, they are gained from sense perception (αἰσθήσεως).

Aristotle has some difficulty in expressing his exact meaning on this score, so he resorts to an analogy. He explains the inductive formation of a universal notion (καθόλου, the "in-general") in terms of a military metaphor. Thus, just as in a general retreat on a battlefield one soldier making a stand (στάντος) soon rallies about him other soldiers until a new battle line is formed, so also, Aristotle says, does one perception make a stand in the mind and soon other percepts of a like kind rally about it until a universal, that is, an "in-general" is formed. In this passage from the last chapter of the *Posterior Analytics* Aristotle does not explain how this process works in detail, other than to add that the human mind or psyche ($\psi v \chi \acute{\eta}$) is so constituted as to be capable of doing this.

In other words, the way our knowledge of universals is "in-duced" or inducted into the mind is by an individual percept coming to stand through sense perception. For example, when I see Callias or Socrates, I always see the *man* Callias or the *man* Socrates, and it is thus that by experiencing men such as Callias and Socrates the universal "man" comes to be firmly established in my mind. Thus since the act of sense perception necessarily involves a universal (Socrates *is* a *man*, and so is Callias), the universal becomes present in the soul with the percept-ion of Socrates or Callias, and other percepts of the same sort can be gathered around this one. Even though Aristotle remains unclear as to the exact process whereby sense perception produces the universal in the mind, he nonetheless insists that it does so, and that the mind is so constituted as to be able to do it.

There is, then, for Aristotle knowledge that is more fundamental than the scientific or demonstrable knowledge, which may be expressed syllogistically. There is, first of all, the quick wit necessary to grasp the connections which may lead to demonstrable scientific knowledge. There is also something more fundamental than this, namely, the process of induction whereby universals are formed from sense experience. But even more basic than these is the mysterious thing Aristotle calls *nous*. This word is often translated by the English word "intuition," with the characteristic ambiguities and confusions necessarily attached to that word. And yet, the inductive process that gains the universals—the "ingenerals," which are materially productive of scientific knowledge—requires this even more fundamental power of "seeing" whereby the first principles of any and every science, the primary premises (ἀρχῆς), are grasped, in such way that scientifically demonstrable knowledge should be possible at all. *Nous* grasps the fundamentals with an immediate and intuitive grasp. And if the power that grasps the middle term connections between propositions is termed "quick wit" (*agchinoia*), then that which grasps the primary premises, without which scientific knowledge and scientific demonstration could not be had, might best be called simply "wit."

This "wit" is not simply "seeing the point" of connection between the major and minor through a middle term, or is it simply "seeing" the universals as they are induced into the mind through sense perception and experience, and allowed to make their stand. It is even more than this. This primary "seeing" grasps the primary truths,[16] the basic premises of any and every science, upon which bases the whole superstructure of scientifically demonstrable knowledge must, indeed, rest.

It may then be entirely true to say, as Descartes will actually say, that the Aristotelian syllogism is itself fundamentally uncreative, that it is not a tool or instrument (an organon in the truly creative sense of that word) for the discovery of new truth. Still, this does not mean that creativity is not involved, and this by necessity, in any process of syllogistic reasoning. In Aristotle's understanding of the matter there is the creativity of seeing the connections of the middle terms without which the formulation of the syllogism would be impossible. Furthermore, there is the creativity on a more sensual level involved in the process of grasping the universals within sense experience. This "seeing," according to Aristotle's analogy, occurs through sense perception, even though it is a "seeing" which is done by the mind. Finally, there is the all-important, creative "seeing" of the primary and basic premises of any and every science, so that the complete structure of scientifically demonstrable knowledge might be built up in the first place. But in all these it is the same fundamental "human wit" (*nous*), whose "quick-wittedness" (*agchinoia*) grasps the connections between propositions in a line of reasoning, forms the universals of knowledge from sense experience, and also grasps the primary premises, the most general concepts, the very idea of any and every science as the most demonstrably known.

One might ask what sort of contribution the organon of Aristotle is able to make toward an understanding of creativity. First of all, he emphasizes the central importance of the mind—whether in its primary grasp of the first principles of each particular science and of science in general, or in its ability to grasp as quickly as possible the connective links between one proposition and the next in a process of reasoning. However, one does not fail to recognize the importance of sense experience in the formation of the universals of experience, as providing the material for the elements connected in the line of demonstrative reasoning.

One of the chief remaining problems arises from the vague explanation that Aristotle gives for the way the universals are formed. He resorts to an analogy, and in the end simply states that the mind is so constituted as to be capable of this process. In many ways the explanation for the sort of creativity involved in this connection between mind and sense had to await the profound analysis of Kant. The important contribution of Aristotle lay in his realization that any organon of discovery necessarily implied an ability to connect related things to each other. This ability to relate and to connect, sometimes in odd and yet in striking fashions, it must be said, lies at the very heart of any creative use of the mind, no matter in what field or discipline.

DESCARTES VS. ARISTOTLE

There is no doubt that René Descartes (1596-1650) was concerned with the problem of discovery in the sciences and also in philosophy. He possessed an eminently creative mind himself, and he was convinced that in the proper study and following of the *Rules for the Direction of the Mind* the "good sense" (*bon sens*), of which all men are endowed, could be extended in the advancement of knowledge in all directions.

What Descartes is saying, in effect, is what any truly creative mind is tempted to say, "Here is the way I discovered new truth; use it, and you too can become creative." Descartes' method is one of the first of what might be called the "cookbook" approaches to creativity. The basis for Descartes' firm conviction on this score is to be found in his belief that the mind is essentially one, in no matter what way or in what direction it may apply its power. All sciences, as he suggests in the first of his *Rules for the Direction of the Mind*, are nothing but *humana scientia*;[18] all are interconnected one with the other (*inter se esse connexas*).[19]

Thus, in opposition to Aristotle, Descartes does not believe that the various sciences can be distinguished from one another in terms of the difference of their subject matters, each one studied in isolation from the rest. For him there is one, and only one, knowing faculty in man, even though that single knowing faculty of the human mind may turn its powers in different directions and toward different objects of study. However, if the mind is essentially one, then there is really only one proper way to use the mind. There is only one method whereby new truth is to be gained, even though that truth may lie in many different areas of study. For if the mind is one, then so is its method. This means that the method that operates as the organon of new discovery in one science should also operate as the organon of discovery in other sciences as well, that is, if it is the true method of the mind.

Hence, for Descartes the first and most important task, if not the only task of philosophy, is to find the right method, namely, to discover the simple and certain rules that will lead to true knowledge of all those things which are able to be known.[20] Indeed, if the search for all truth were attempted without method, then the truth would likely never be attained; and even if it were somehow gained, it would be largely by luck or by accident, rather than by design. Truth gained by chance rather than by art would be worse than no truth gained, as Descartes suggests in Rule X.[21]

For Descartes there are basically two sources of human knowledge: we know through experience (*per experientiam*) and through deduction (*deductionem*).[22] Concerning this latter source of knowledge Descartes doubts very much that people make mistakes in reasoning or in logic. He insists that it is not so much by faculty inference (*mala illatione*) that the mind is deceived and easily led astray as much as by experience falsely and rashly judged. The mind, Descartes is convinced, is never deceived if the object in question is precisely intuited (*intueatur*).[23] In other words, if man uses this power of intuition he possesses, he cannot go wrong. What is this mysterious power to which Descartes refers?

In the first place he cautions his readers that they are to follow the Latin meanings of the words most strictly. Hence, when he says intuition is the pure and attentive "seeing" that the mind performs, free from any element of doubt in its conceiving, then those things which are intuited or "seen into" (*in-tueor*) will be seen and understood clearly and without the shadow of a doubt. Thus as Descartes says, in effect, in Rule IX, "attend, attend, and attend, until you see"; and if one truly attends, fixing by attention the strong light of intuition upon the object in quest, he shall see, Descartes promises.

This fundamental seeing is also a necessary part of any process of deduction. For Descartes things can be necessarily concluded only from other things that are more certainly known. Even more than this, in any chain of inference it is impossible to intuit the whole of that chain of inference all at once. Not even all the immediate links of the chain of inference, upon which their necessary connection must depend, are or could be intuited as immediately present evidence. They are put together by intuition in their proper order of connection and held together by memory.[24]

It is easy to appreciate the difference in "method" in Descartes and in Aristotle on this score of deduction. Aristotle's logic depends very much upon an "intuition" of the mediate links, the connective middle terms. Certainly, in any complex line of reasoning this might tend to prove cumbersome. One should, indeed, intuit the first principles by intuition, and gain the conclusions by means of deduction; however, one might easily be led astray in the process, since the distance from the original intuition or previous deductions might prove too great or too difficult to follow. It is for this reason that Descartes reduces all deduction to intuition. He attempts to collapse the whole deductive sequence into a unit by means of *enumeration*. This enumeration and its importance for the right use of the method become the subject of the whole of the lengthy Rule VIII. There must be an absolutely exhaustive enumeration of all that might possibly have bearing upon the issue at hand. This rule of enumeration, it might be mentioned, constitutes one of the four essential rules of method which Descartes synthesizes from the doctrines of the *Regulae,* as he sets forth the essence of the method in his *Discourse on Method.*[25]

In the first of these rules Descartes insists that only what is clearly and obviously true is to be accepted. The basis for this rule was contained already in Descartes' notion of intuition as something conceived without doubt (*non dubium conceptum*). In fact, it was fundamentally on this score that Descartes was so critical of the logic of the Schoolmen, and the "torments of their probable syllogisms." He granted that this study of logic might be good practice for the wits (*ingenia*) of youth; however, in accordance with the right use of the mind through the method, the false must never be accepted as true.[26]

The second and third rules, as they are given in the *Discourse,* constitute the very heart of Descartes' method. Accordingly, the problem must be broken down into its constituent elements, in order that it may be studied more easily part by part. In this way we begin with what is simplest and most easily known (that is, "seen"),[27] proceeding from the simple to the most complex. And to this he adds the words ". . . et supposant même de l'ordre entre ceux qui ne se précèdent point naturellement les uns les autres."[28] What

Descartes means by "supposing an order" when a definite order is not apparent, he makes clear in Rule X of the *Regulae*. He takes the example of attempting to break a code or a cipher. When faced with a coded message, we do not readily recognize an order, only a mass of meaningless letters or numbers or symbols. No order appears; hence in such cases we make (*fingimus*) an order, a hypothetical order where a natural one is not to be found.[29] Indeed, as Descartes says, it is not always easy to think an order (*in ordine excogitando*), and yet once it is known or recognized (*cognoscendo*), it is easy to make others "see" it.[30]

It is exactly on this point that Descartes is so critical of the ancients. For from his study of some of the ancient mathematicians he is convinced that they knew something of the true method that he was seeking. This he could discern from the very nature of their discoveries. But for some reason these ancient geometricians did not pass on to posterity the actual method whereby they made their new discoveries. Descartes finds something of this true and "universal mathesis" (the method) in Pappo and Diophanto, who could have made their discoveries only by the use of such a method. Descartes actually accuses them of bad faith; they deliberately and "with pernicious cunning" suppressed the method. Why they should have done such a dastardly thing, leaves Descartes with the surmise that the method was so simple that it might easily have become vulgarized by others. Possibly, however, they wanted to be admired as clever.[31]

Descartes is very severe with those ancient mathematicians who exhibited their genius in the results they produced, but who refused to show the true method whereby they achieved such results. They left us with their findings, but did not (or would not) pass on the method whereby these findings were made; and in this lay their true genius. However, if Descartes is severe with the ancient mathematicians, he is even more severe with the "logicians."

The philosopher's attack upon logic is many-pronged. Reduced to its essentials, his argument against the logicians or "dialecticians" is that their whole approach is essentially uncreative. As he explains in Rule X, the dialecticians are totally incapable of forming any true conclusion by their logical art (*arte*), unless the material (*materiam*) from which they draw their various conclusions be already known before. This means that they perceive absolutely nothing new (*nihil novi*) from their logical formulations. They simply set forth (*exponendos*) more conveniently truths that were already known and that have been obtained from different sources. Hence their art belongs more properly to rhetoric than to philosophy.[32]

Whether Descartes' attack upon the "dialecticians" represents an attack or even a fair criticism of the practices of latter-day Aristotelians is beside the point. The central point which Descartes makes, it would seem, could hardly be disputed by Aristotle. The "logical art" depends upon material of some sort. For Aristotle this "material" came through sense experience and via induction. However, he would insist against Descartes that there is an element of creativity in a "seeing" of the connective links between terms of propositions. Otherwise, how should they become linked together at all to produce a line of reasoning or of thought?

Descartes, on the other hand, refuses to distinguish between two extremes and a middle term in any process of reasoning or logic.[33] His substitute for the syllogism lies not so much in "seeing" the relation between the connective middle terms as in the process of constant and exhaustive enumeration. By means of such enumeration he attempts to collapse the elements of the inference into a shape that can be readily intuited as a whole. It can be intuited as a whole because all the elements forming that whole have already been broken up into their constituent parts. Descartes insists that if this were not done, that is, if one were to attempt to intuit the singulars separately and individually, the multiplicity itself might stand in the way. Thus it is that Descartes suggests that those elements which do not require immediate attention might best be retained in the memory.[34] For since the simplest and most absolute elements are marked out for the certain and sure starting point, then those elements which are to come later in their proper order must be held in the memory until they are needed. They must, however, be reviewed and enumerated. For in order to see what the problem is, it is necessary to determine what is known and understood, unknown and not understood. Descartes cannot emphasize enough the importance of enumeration.

In Rule VIII Descartes compares the task of forming his new method with the problem of forging new instruments. The mind is one, and hence the method that the mind develops and applies to various subjects or problems must be one as well. But how is one to establish the method proper to the human mind when all one has to work with is the human mind itself? Descartes would suggest that essentially the same sort of problem faced primitive man, namely, how to make tools without the tools necessary to make those first primitive tools. At first those tools or instruments from which more refined tools could be developed were bound to be crude. Descartes compares this problem of making tools without tools to that of fashioning the proper organon (tool) or method of the mind for discovering truth. As he observes, nothing is more important than the investigation of human knowing (*humana cognitio*). This is, presumably, the "crude instrument" that must be sharpened up to refashion the mind into the refined tool of discovery. Thus Descartes can say that in this investigation of human knowing are contained both the tools of human knowing, and, with a little refinement, the whole of the method itself.[35]

This concern with the theory of knowledge—with the careful analysis of man's "tools" for knowing and discovery, so much the concern of modern philosophy—may be seen to take its cue exactly from these lines in Descartes' thought. In fact, given the philosopher's presupposition, already noted above, that the mind is basically and essentially one, the investigation of this basic and indispensable tool becomes the primary, if not the only task of philosophy. For if the mind is one, then the ideal method, namely, the most fruitful means whereby the mind would come to know truth, must be one also. It is in this light that Descartes' somewhat severe criticisms of the ancient geometers and logicians must be seen. These geometers left mankind with their results, but failed to leave the method whereby they attained them. The logicians, with all the skill of their dialectical art, only furnished exercise for the mind. The geometers concealed their method; the method of the logicians was simply sterile, possibly good exercise for young minds, though Descartes would suggest the exclusive study of mathematics as a better preparatory training for the method.[36]

Reduced to its essentials, what exactly is the method advocated by Descartes? Often after outlining one of the features or elements of the method, Descartes will underscore the fact that this or that feature is the "essence" or most important element of the method. Upon a more careful study of Descartes' method, that is, with all the unnecessary repetitions and apparent contradictions removed, it might be reduced to two essential points. One must first divide the problem into its constituent parts, noting what is known and understood, unknown and not understood. In thus breaking the problem into pieces one succeeds in creating a "chaos." Then the task becomes one of "ordering" the chaos, beginning with those elements most simply and most surely known. In this process of ordering the chaos one may, if it is expedient, introduce a hypothetical order where a real order is not readily apparent. It is in this sense that Descartes says all explanations in physics must be hypothetical, even though all such hypothetical orderings must be mechanical, this being stipulated for speculative or metaphysical reasons.

To sum up, Descartes' method is relatively simple. It consists essentially of a chaos and an ordering of that chaos. However, the matrix for such an ordering must be a single and incontrovertible certainty. And it is on this score that one of the elements of Descartes' method may actually run counter to the creative use of the mind. The "creation" of the chaos certainly presents no problem. The problem need not be torn down into pieces, for this generally takes place by itself, particularly after a great deal of time, thought, and energy has been devoted to a specific problem or field of study. One need not bother creating a chaos; this creates itself, if only through the constant "enumeration" which Descartes demands. A much more serious difficulty is the necessary first step in the process or ordering, whether that ordering be fictitious or real, namely, finding something to begin with which is most simple and most certain.

Certitude, it must be admitted, remains something of a Cartesian bugbear. Indeed many writers—for example,

Poincaré, as we shall see—attest to the feeling of certainty and satisfaction that tends to follow immediately upon the solution of a particular problem, be it artistic or scientific. However, to require such certitude as a necessary starting point could lead to difficulties. For instance, to demand that one begin at a point of absolute certitude, no matter how basic and fundamental it may be conceived, will generally require that all the other elements or parts be marshaled or ordered in accordance with that primary conviction of certitude. And this can, in turn, represent an a priori arrangement of those elements in an order preordained by the original and certain starting point; it can even require a "tailoring" of those elements or facts that follow. The feeling that one is correct, and that there is no other solution to a particular problem, may come after the completing of the ordering process. When it comes before and is required as a necessary condition for beginning, a dangerous apriorism can be the result.

Certitude is, indeed, associated with creativity. It should not, however, be demanded at the very start of the process. For even when one is absolutely convinced that the solution to the scientific or artistic problem to which one has arrived is the only possible one, it does not take long before other facts from the "chaos"—possibly pointed out by others—re-enter the picture, causing doubt not only about the solution gained but even about the absolutely certain starting point.

Much more important, however, is Descartes' suggestion that it may be useful to introduce a hypothetical order where a real one is not apparent. This means that it may be advisable to set up certain experimental models and test them out to determine which one may prove the most valuable. However, the testing of such hypothetical orderings does not constitute Descartes' method, nor does it necessarily represent creativity. The element of creativity would rather consist in the discovery of the hypothesis itself, the preliminary ordering of the chaos of facts and data.

There is, nevertheless, a more fundamental question involved here, and that is the whole question of method itself, as well as the relation of method to discovery. Descartes' belief that the mind is essentially one means that the method which the mind makes use of must be one as well. The mind, indeed, may be essentially one; however, the many different problems and areas of study to which the mind may turn or direct its attention are clearly many and various. And it may not be entirely fair to the data of the many and various problems and disciplines to which the mind may direct itself to demand a single and solitary method. In other words, it may be perfectly true that Descartes' method worked eminently well in the discovery of analytic geometry; however, that does not mean that the method will work equally well when applied to problems of psychology or metaphysics.

What, after all, is a method? It is a "way after" something (from the Greek μετὰ, meaning "after," and ὁδός, a "road"). However, the path which a person takes, the road he follows, the means he uses—all this is governed, at least to some extent, by the destination or goal that he wishes to attain. There are different ways of getting to Europe, but swimming is not one of them. There are different methods for cutting the lawn, but using a pair of scissors would hardly be considered. The problem with discovery, Descartes rightly saw, was primarily one of forging more refined tools from more rough and crude ones. Originally, the only means of crossing a body of water was to swim. However, a floating log and a broad stick used as a paddle might be a better method of crossing. The tools that help make this new method of transport have to be forged from tools that are even more rough and crude. This necessary forging of new tools in order to gain a new and creative solution to the particular problem at hand, it might be suggested, must be done anew in each and every case. For in every case the problems to be solved will be different, if only because of the context in which they are encountered.

The mind may, indeed, be one, but the problems and tasks to which the mind may address itself are not, and new approaches and new methods, new tools, must constantly be forged and refined so as to deal with them. This is, in truth, one of the problems in being creative: it is not simply a matter of creating new solutions with old tools and methods, but also one of creating the new tools and methods necessary to gain these new solutions. Thus the choice of one overbearing, rigorously applied method may actually deter, rather than encourage, creativity. A particular method may have an immediate use here and now; nevertheless, universal and eternal validity should hardly be accorded to it. And its rigorous and single-minded use may actually kill that which it is intended to foster.

Bacon and the New Organon

In many ways Francis Bacon (1561-1626) is the philosopher of the modern age. The public philosophy of our scientific and technological age is Baconian. For it was Bacon who provided the West with the *new* organon to replace the old, worn-out tool or instrument supposedly fashioned by Aristotle and his followers.

Reduced to its essentials Bacon's philosophy is a very simple one—and considered at face value, a very pious one.

It might be compressed into three short sentences, two commands and one theological reason. The two commands are: (1) make tools; (2) subdue nature; and (3) the theological reason is because God demands it of us. He finds the basis for his philosophical program in Genesis (1:28) where God says, "Be fruitful, multiply, fill the earth, and subdue it. . . ." Bacon takes this divine injunction most seriously. Man is meant, indeed destined and commanded by God, to gain dominion over nature.

With this theological basis firmly established, and out of the way, Bacon can proceed to the means necessary to lead to the subduing of nature. And on this score he finds that a total reform must be undertaken of the old organon, the old tool or instrument, for the gaining of new learning and ideas as fashioned by the Aristotelians. Thus noting that the then existing sciences, logic included, in no way provide a new method for invention and discovery, he wishes to propose and to fashion a new tool, a *Novum Organum*.

The reason why Bacon considers the tool of logic as useless lies in the fact that syllogisms are made up of propositions, propositions of words; but since words are the symbols of notions, if these notions are confused or rashly abstracted from things, then everything collapses like a house of cards. Hence the only true hope lies in induction.[37]

Bacon points up the fact that the beginning of any true process of discovery must start with the sensible particulars of experience, which are gained by means of induction. With this Aristotle would have heartily agreed; it was exactly with induction that any process of new knowledge had to begin. However, Bacon means something slightly different by induction than did Aristotle. For Bacon induction implies the slow and painstaking amassing of data and information until enough has been amassed to provide a general conclusion. Induction, as he says, takes its axioms from the sense and from particulars, gradually ascending to axioms until finally the most general axioms of all are attained.[38]

The difference between Aristotle and Bacon on the meaning of induction may appear insignificant, but it is crucial. And that difference, it may be said, lies in a thing called "form." For Aristotle in the induction of the universal from sense experience a "form" (the universal) is necessarily contained; otherwise, according to Aristotle's way of thinking, it would be impossible to recognize *man* (the universal) in sensibly particular men such as Socrates or Callias. For Bacon, on the other hand, nature must not be dissected into its constituent parts by abstraction, but rather materially. "Forms," Bacon insists, are nothing but the fabrications or fictions (*commenta*) of the human mind.[39]

Thus even though one may translate Aristotle's *epagoge* by the Latinized word "induction," this induction from sense particulars does not at all mean the same thing in Bacon and in Aristotle. For Bacon the "form" or universal concept is not in-duced out of a field of sense perception in the way that for Aristotle one soldier "makes a stand" on the field of battle and soon other soldiers begin to gather about him making a new formation. For Bacon it is matter, not form, which ought rather to be considered and studied.

Bacon's insistence that nature must be considered physically and materially, rather than by abstraction, is thoroughly in keeping with his whole conception of philosophy. Thus in his work *Of the Dignity and Advancement of Learning* Bacon gives a division and classification of the sciences. In its outward appearance it has all the characteristics of a traditional classification of human knowledge. In Book II of the work Bacon divides "human doctrine" ac-

cording to its bases (*sedes*) in the rational soul: thus corresponding to the memory its history; to the imagination
(*phantasiam*), poetry; and to reason, philosophy.[40]

Bacon further divides philosophy into three doctrines,
nature, God, and man, drawing a parallel with rays of light.
Thus nature strikes the human intellect by direct ray (*radio
directo*); God by a ray refracted (*radio refracto*); and that
part of philosophy concerned with man by a reflex ray
(*radio reflexo*). He insists, however, that these various par-
titions of the sciences represent so many limbs of a tree
joined together to one trunk. This trunk, which must be
understood as the mother of all the rest of the sciences,
Bacon calls the universal science (*scientia universalis*), first
philosophy, or wisdom. This science contains the axioms that
are common and fundamental to all the sciences, not simply
to particular ones.[41]

Bacon, however, seeks an inquiry that is more firm and
more established; he seeks the laws that are according to
nature. And these he finds in what he calls natural philosophy. Bacon distinguishes two parts of natural philosophy,
a speculative part and a practical part. The speculative
part of natural philosophy attempts to probe the "guts"
(*viscera*) of nature; and on this score one may recall Bacon's
remark in the *Novum Organum* that nature should be dissected materially rather than by abstraction. The operative
part of natural philosophy attempts to form and shape nature as upon an anvil,[42] which was, one may recall, the
divine command Bacon takes most seriously, namely, the
subjection and domination of nature by man. The operative
part of physics Bacon calls "mechanics," which in his way
of looking at things is often worked out with the help of
mathematics.[43] The speculative part of physics is subjected
to further complicated divisions and subdivisions.

The role of metaphysics in the Baconian scheme of things proves to be extremely limited. First philosophy, that is, the science of the most general axiomata, must, he insists, be entirely disjoined from metaphysics. Nor does he accept the traditional areas of metaphysics. For example, any consideration of the "transcendentals" (being, thing, truth, beauty, and so forth) he holds to be without foundation. Neither should metaphysics be confused with what he calls natural theology, which concerns itself with God, Angels, Spirits, and the Good. What, then, is left for the study of metaphysics? And Bacon answers, "Beyond nature, surely, nothing."[44] Metaphysics, as becomes clear, is neither really nor conceptually distinct from physics. It merely deals with the more abstract and stable parts of nature.

When one comes to the end of Bacon's long and unnecessarily involved division and classification of the sciences, one discovers that for Bacon there is basically only one science, and that science is a purely naturalistic and materialistic physics. And only those sciences are to be considered "humanly" scientific which are somehow connected with this broadly conceived notion of physics. There may be phases to this all-embracing naturalism; but natural philosophy remains essentially one for Bacon, not only in its "speculative" side, but also in that to which the speculative is and must necessarily be ordained, namely, the operative.

This conclusion regarding the basic unity of Bacon's scheme of the sciences is born out in his metaphor of the pyramid. Thus at the base of the pyramid of Bacon's all-embracing philosophy is natural history; the next stage is physics; and immediately above this (*vertici proximum*) is metaphysics. The top point of the pyramid he conceives to be the ultimate and summary law of nature, whose inquiry by man, he feels, is doubtful of success.[45]

The only distinction that Bacon really draws in his classification of the sciences is between theology and philosophy. Theology he leaves to the Divines, though he is not loathe to use a revealed truth of inspired theology to back up the overbearing drive of his philosophy for a complete control over physical nature. The divine command to subdue nature Bacon observes most religiously. The operative side of his physics is nothing more than this. And the speculative side is less an attempt to understand the nature of the physical universe than to provide the sort of technical and scientific knowledge necessary to gain control over nature, subduing it, and bringing it under the dominion of man. It is with good reason that Bacon is called the philosopher of the modern technological age!

However, there is one aspect of Bacon's philosophy which, more than any other, contributed to the crisis of our scientific and technological age, and hence also to that phenomenon we have characterized as the crisis of creativity. And that is Bacon's attitude toward poetry. Thus tucked away neatly in his division and classification of the sciences was the remark that poetry has its seat in the imagination (*Phantasia*), and is nothing else but the concocting of stories and fables, to which there is nothing conforming in the nature of things.[46] Clearly poetry can have no part in natural philosophy, that is, science. As he says, speaking of narrative poetry, since the sensible world is inferior in dignity to the rational soul, this poetry appears to expand upon those things history denies, in order thereby to satisfy the soul with shadows, when more solid things cannot be attained.[47] Poetry and the arts are, for Bacon, nothing but a diversion for the mind, through the free play of the imagination or phantasy. It has nothing to do with the sort of scientific understanding which is to gain technological control over nature.

In his concern with a new organon, a new tool or instrument for learning and discovery, Bacon manifests a spirit akin to that of Descartes, namely, a strong interest in method. In an age in which technical advances with far-reaching economic and social consequences were coming on the scene, Bacon felt that a new philosophy was needed in order to keep pace with such new technical inventions and, possibly, even to assist in their creation and implementation. And yet, in many ways, the organon or method which he proposes rejects, as outside the interest of his thoroughly naturalistic physics, one of the truly catalytic elements necessary for creativity in the sciences, namely, the poetic and artistic development of the imagination. For him the imagination or phantasy is simply the seat of poetry and has nothing to do with the physical reality that is of interest to the scientist in his drive to understand and control nature. In this, one can recognize the description, if not the actual origin, of the so-called problem of the two cultures, that is, the literary and the humanistic, the scientific and the technical. Bacon is witness to this separation, if he is not its actual cause. And this separation, I am convinced, has been as disastrous for science in the years since Bacon as it has been for the humanities.

The new method or organon that Bacon proposes labors under the same difficulties that any and every method, as a tool for discovery, labors. Methods can be extremely useful. For a method provides a means of handling a vast array of facts and data; it is able to reduce the confusion of too much material to manageable proportions. In a sense, of course, a method as a means of discovery represents a way of pre-channeling, of prejudging this vast array of facts and material to be handled and to be put in some definite form or structure. And this is, of course, one of the dangers present in the choice of a single, overbearing method. It can prejudice an honest and careful approach to the particular problems themselves. This we have already noted in relation to Descartes and his method. The choice of a particular method may be creatively conceived; however, if it is *creatively* conceived it will attempt to conform itself to the data or problem in question, not to imagined set categories of a method forged by the human mind. Each problem is unique, which means that it is peculiar to its own data. A predetermined method can prejudge, and hence prejudice any truly creative solution to the problem.

Nevertheless, the problem of method in Descartes, as well as in modern philosophy and in scientific theory, is radically different from the problem of method in Bacon. A method is an organon, a tool, an instrument. If the goal and purpose of that tool or instrument is the control of nature, which is the fundamental drive behind the whole of Bacon's philosophy, then the method or instrument needed to accomplish this must be invented. A method is a means to discovery, but when the end is less discovery than invention in order to control, a radical shift in the meaning of method has occurred. Method is no longer a means for discovery in order to understand, but literally a tool for control. It is no accident that for Bacon the operative part of natural philosophy, the only science he recognizes, is mechanics, and that any speculative part to this one all-embracing science exists solely in order to contribute to his naturalistic physics or mechanics. Bacon's method, the organ or tool to control nature, is nothing more than the machine. Discovery in the sciences is strictly for the control of nature, and it is the machine which represents the ideal tool for this control.

It is not without reason that Bacon is called the father of our modern technological age.

3

The Machine and the Crisis

There are many aspects to the phenomenon we have chosen to call the crisis of creativity but, it seems to me, the single element that has most quickly brought the crisis to a head is the greater and greater automation of business and industry in our society. This ever growing development of the tools and machines of industry is certainly in keeping with Bacon's vision, as we have seen, though it has certainly advanced far beyond anything ever dreamed of by Bacon.

Not that automation and the growth and use of machines as tools by man are anything essentially new. Technological progress on an ever increasing scale, and even in its present form, has been with us at least since the time of the Industrial Revolution, and probably even before. And certainly it would be incorrect to infer simply from the great influence technological progress has had upon Western culture, that there is anything *per se* evil about automation. In fact, many of the benefits of automation are distinctly humane. For one thing, the use of a tool or a machine can provide man with a greater amount of leisure, which, as has been often observed, is the basis of culture. Such leisure, it might be added, is also essential for creativity. And it is for this reason that the crisis of creativity may not be identified with the problem of how to keep the unemployed occupied or how to make a more meaningful and constructive use of the greater amount of free time made available by automation. The crisis of creativity is hardly as simple as the problem of how to keep from being bored. Rather than simply filling free time, creativity requires it.

There are, after all, specifically human benefits to automation. Turning screws on an automobile assembly line, the same screws day in and day out, is not necessarily to be considered a humane ideal. With the technological advances of automation the working man need no longer be a mere component in the machine that he operates, a mere part of the large industrial complex within which he labors. Indeed, he may lose his job, as he is replaced by a machine designed to do more efficiently and more quickly the function that he had performed. However, this may only mean that the particular task he was performing was purely mechanical in function, hardly to be considered as work ideal for him as a human person. And even as certain jobs are automated out of existence, other jobs are created in the servicing, building, and programming of the new machines that may have replaced him. The problem for the individual in such cases is largely one of social mobility; in other words, the economic, educational, and familial problems attendant upon any radical shift in employment.

However, it is not automation in this form which has brought the crisis of creativity to a head. The crisis of creativity is not simply the result of the enforced leisure of idleness and unemployment. The crisis of creativity arises from a different sort of automation. It arises when the minor executive in a large business or corporation finds that the company which has employed him—possibly for many years

—to make decisions in business and industry no longer has any need of him; a machine has been "hired" that can make decisions more quickly and make predictions more accurately than could the executive.

Here the crisis of creativity comes to a head. For with this kind of "automation" the machine has trespassed upon a domain, namely, that of judging and decision-making, which man has always considered to be his alone. It is this sort of "job-replacement" that not only produces personal and family and hence social crises of great moment, but is a "crisis" in the truly Greek sense of that word. It is a crisis touching decision, even man's decision-making ability. When man the decision-maker is replaced by a machine, the decisive consequences, whether social, personal, or even philosophical, can hardly be ignored.

The use of tools, instruments, and machines is not, as we have said, something essentially new in the history of man. Man can cup his hand and use it to scoop up dirt, or to gouge a hole out of the earth, or to move dirt or other material from one place to another. However, man soon found that by making the "cup" out of some very hard substance, first wood or stone but later metal, and by attaching this piece of flattened metal to a wooden pole, this new tool, which he called a shovel, was able to move greater amounts of dirt or material from one place to another more quickly and with even less effort. The process could be extended even further. It was possible to make an even larger and stronger cup, powered not by the energy of human muscle but with energy produced by steam or an internal combustion engine; and with the addition of steel cables and strong steel arms, man had an instrument, a tool, a machine capable of moving even greater amounts of dirt or stone yet more quickly and efficiently.

By taking this same process and multiplying it many times over in all the areas of human industry, the modern technological age was born. Modern man may have thought that he saw an end to this process of expanding mechanization. He may have thought that there were inherent limits to machines. However, he soon discovered that machines could be made to make yet other machines, while man simply looked on.

These developments did not yet disturb man's conviction of his superiority over the machines that he made. After all, he was the one who first formed the ideas for such machines, designed and built them to lighten his tasks. Thus when he invented the calculating machine, which was able to perform sums, division, subtraction, and a host of other mathematical operations with speed and accuracy that far surpassed man in this regard, the machines had overcome yet another area of his workaday world. This did not particularly disturb man. After all, he had made these new machines, or at least the machines that made the machines, and so on. Besides, this only proved that man's intelligence and genius consisted in much more than in doing sums. This he had thought all along, even from grammar school.

Then a technological innovation, namely, the discovery of the transistor, and a theoretical element, namely, the binomial number system, combined to produce a new kind of machine. This was all in perfect accord with the Baconian philosophy. There were, after all, two parts to the one science, a speculative and an operative part. Further, Bacon had always considered mathematics as a sort of appendage to the philosophy of nature. It was conceived as an auxiliary tool both of the speculative and operative parts of the doctrine of nature.[1]

However, it was at this point that the new machines

created a crisis. For the machines, as programmed, were able to take into account vast quantities of information, store much of it in their "memory banks," to be called forth on demand; and from this vast store of information make judgments and even project decisions in terms of the information it possessed.

Man could, of course, console himself with the fact that the machines had to be programmed, and that the "decisions" that were made depended to a great extent upon the information he fed into them.

However, it was soon possible to build computers that seemed to possess a "nervous system" similar to that of man. It appeared as though they were able to "learn": they could make decisions on the basis of decisions made in the past.[2] Their knowledge was cumulative, which meant that in the making of decisions that required the enumeration of a vast array of facts and data, they were superior to man.

Not only could the machines, in certain cases, make better and more accurate decisions and projections than a man, but purpose could be built into the machines. And with this invasion of the living and projective character of human intelligence by the machines, man was thrown back on the last line of defense. For with this, machines could be developed which would program themselves.

In many ways it is at this point the Baconian philosophy of modern science reached and found its denouement. And many other philosophies, such as positivism and naturalism, as also psychologies, such as behaviorism, spawned by the same scientific movement that gave rise to Bacon, and to which movement he had so strongly contributed, faced similar crises. For as the machines took over and performed more and more of the functions that before had been considered the preserves of human intelligence alone, the philosophies and psychologies—which explained human intelligence solely in terms of mechanical functions conceived after the model of the machine—had the difficult if not impossible task of explaining the unique characteristic that made human intelligence not simply different from the machine, so that it could *create* the machine in the first place, but also one of explaining what made human intelligence capable of explaining itself to itself in terms of machine-like functions.

This is certainly a part of the crisis of creativity, although it might more appropriately be called the crisis of all those explanations of man and of the nature of human knowing that have been conceived solely in terms of the sort of mechanical and naturalistic functions espoused by Bacon. Nevertheless it also raises a larger question which is troubling a greater number of psychologists, philosophers, and even scientists. What is it man possesses that makes him better than the machine he makes and programs, or which he makes to program itself? Or to ask the same question in a slightly different way: If the machines are able to "make decisions," then how does man's decision-making ability differ from that of the machine? Or, if the machine is able to "think," then what is meant by human thinking?

The key word that psychologists have hit upon most recently to explain the special function of human intelligence that makes man superior to the things he creates, whether machines or whatever, is *creativity*. This must also play a part in what we have termed the crisis of creativity. For if many of the functions that philosophers and psychologists thought man alone could perform can be done more quickly and efficiently by machines designed for the same purpose, then it must mean that man's true genius must lie in his intelligent power to create. And it means that the development and perfection of this power must receive ever greater attention in education, that is, if man is even to proceed ahead of the machines he builds and programs or programs to program themselves. Thus one may note in recent years the number of books and articles in the area of psychology dealing with the difference between intelligence and creativity.[3] The studies upon which these works are based point out that many of the children who are very high in intelligence (as measured by I.Q. tests) are not necessarily high in creativity; and those who are judged high in creativity tests do not necessarily achieve high scores in tests for intelligence.

The results of these tests in intelligence and creativity quotients, however, could be interpreted in a different way. It could mean that the tests which purportedly measured intelligence have simply failed to measure the creative factor in human intelligence. In fact, one might argue that many I.Q. tests were set up in such fashion as to measure human intelligence as though the mind of man were only a more elaborate electronic computer. Most intelligence tests are based upon a series of increasingly difficult mathematical, mechanical, and verbal analogies. The element of speed in "seeing" the points of connection was all-important. The tests claimed to test intelligence. However, what they succeeded in testing, more often than not, was the ability of simple, basic judging, in the quickest possible time. They tested the ability to make and see connections. They tested, one might say, the "quick wit" of Aristotle, the art of seeing connections quickly. They tested a logical facility, which, it might be pointed out, could be performed more quickly and efficiently by a machine, if it were properly programmed. The conclusion was inescapable: either the machines had higher I.Q.'s than people; or it would be necessary to find another quality in human intelligence (namely, creativity) to account for man's poor showing against the machines, and yet his ability to create the machines.

The greater speed and accuracy of the computers in making logical judgments and in solving logical puzzles have also tended to put certain modern logicians, who had completely identified philosophy with logic, in a similarly delicate position. For if the machines could be programmed in such way as to work out complex logical puzzles with a quickness and accuracy far surpassing that of man, then this must mean there is more to thinking and more to philosophy than working out logical puzzles. It would appear that Aristotle was entirely correct in leaving logic outside his division and classification of philosophy. And it would appear that those philosophers who reduced philosophy to nothing more than logic betrayed philosophy (and themselves) into the hands of the machines.

There are, then, many aspects to the phenomenon we have termed the crisis of creativity. In some ways it is simply the crisis of man in the machine age. And certainly it was only when the development of the machine age had run its course that man was suddenly made to realize that, if human intelligence is interpreted in terms primarily mechanical, to be measured mathematically, and if machines are able to assume more and more of the mechanical functions of human intelligence, then there had to be something more to human intelligence than the mechanistic explanations of intelligence had themselves allowed for. And with this there was also a crisis in those philosophies which had either caused, or had been spawned by, the rapid growth and full development of a mechanized civilization.

One may also recognize one of the fundamental causes

of the crisis of creativity in the rejection of the element of the "poetic," both by Bacon and others. It may be true that poetry has very little to do with scientific objectivity; however, that does not mean that it has nothing whatever to do with scientific discovery. Bacon understood poetry and literature as but the escape of reason from reality into the imagination. He was right to an extent. It is possible to escape, at least momentarily, from an involvement with one's own problems by identifying oneself with the problems and causes of the hero or chief protagonist of a play or a novel. It is equally true that literature is different from the spirit and attitude of scientific objectivity. It is hardly "scientific" to throw oneself into the particular story or play, identifying oneself with the characters as they are created on the stage or as they arise out of the printed page and form themselves in the imagination. Nonetheless, this is not the nature or the primary function of literature, and as we shall see later, this quality or attitude of personal involvement and of identification is essential to creativity, not simply in the arts but also in the sciences.

This does not mean that the so-called problem of the two cultures is simply the problem of the artist in a technological age. This rejection of the "poetic" element by Bacon is possibly even more disastrous for the ongoing of science as well. For how can science itself be truly creative if analogous forms of creativity in the arts and in the humanities are ignored or set aside in the name of "scientific objectivity?" Indeed, there is no "creative" way to read scientific instruments and gauges. However, reading instruments and gauges is not all there is to science.

This should not be interpreted as a plea for greater emphasis on the *artes liberales* in our schools of science and technology—although I am convinced that if science is to be creative, it cannot safely ignore creativity in the nonscientific domains of art and the humanities. In the words of the early German romantic Friedrich von Schlegel, *alle Wissenschaft soll Kunst werden*, the sciences must become more poetic.[4]

Ultimately, one may say, the crisis of creativity is simply the eternal crisis which is man himself. It is the crisis that man eternally faces in attempting to find his place not only in the world of his own creation, but also in a world which is not of his own creation. Man must come to terms with both of these "worlds," even though he may be held responsible only for that world which is of his own making. Man is responsible for what he has made, and, at least to some extent, for what he has made of himself. This is why, at root, the crisis of creativity is the crisis of man himself. For what man has made and has made of himself can destroy him.

This is, in the last analysis, the message of existentialism. This philosophy arose in direct opposition to a society, civilization, and view of human life mechanistically conceived. Existentialism insisted upon the importance of the individual man and upon individual man's responsibility for what he does or fails to do. However, existentialism did not go far enough. It analyzed the position of man in his age, but instead of proposing a means for changing that world, existentialism counseled resignation. Oftentimes this resignation was little more than a grimly stoical acceptance of the absurd. It represented defeatism, and in its most extreme forms it advocated, in effect, a philosophy of despair. In many ways existentialism represented a denial of man's basic human power to create. He was held ultimately responsible for the mess he makes and has made of the world and of himself, and then he was denied any means or set of values that might assist him in guiding the tremendous power within himself to create, namely, his human freedom. In its way existentialism also ministered to the crisis of creativity; it recognized the monster but stoically accepted death at its hands, having given up all hope of survival.

It is for these and other reasons, many of which will become apparent only as we proceed, that it will be necessary to return to a consideration of man and the creative capacities of his intelligence. For it is only through a consideration of elements, aspects, and climate necessary for the process of creativity that the crisis of creativity can in any measure be met.

4

The Unconscious and Creativity

If creativity and the crisis it has provoked are to be understood, then the relation between the unconscious and the creative process must be explored. But in attempting to assess the important part which I am convinced the unconscious plays in the process of creativity, we must avoid certain misconceptions regarding the nature of the unconscious. And in this area misconceptions can easily occur. For by definition we are unconscious of the operations of the unconscious. And thus the only way in which the unconscious may be analyzed and the operations, which are performed unconsciously, reconstructed is as they manifest themselves in consciousness.

Nevertheless, this key element in the creative process is not as impervious to analysis as it may at first sight appear. Through various phenomena, which we shall note and study in this section, man is made aware of the existence of such a "faculty" and also of some of its workings. Nothing, I think, is gained by ignoring the role played by the unconscious, particularly in the creative process, simply because of the difficulties posed by such an analysis.

One of the difficulties in dealing with the unconscious lies in the approach to be used. That approach can neither be purely rationalistic nor purely empirical. It cannot be purely rationalistic because of the "irrational" character of the unconscious in many of its operations. On the other hand, the approach to the unconscious cannot be simply empirical; its operations are not directly measurable or scientifically observable in the strict sense of those words.

Nor can the approach to the unconscious be purely phenomenological. We may, indeed, take a phenomenological approach to creativity or to the crisis of creativity; however, insofar as phenomenology represents an eidetic science of the data of pure consciousness and reduced experience, the unconscious would of necessity remain outside any such consideration. And certainly any mode of psychological introspection would be of little help in this regard. For when a person looks into his unconscious, all he sees is *nothing*. This may, indeed, be a way of understanding the unconscious, that is, as a "nothing." Nevertheless, it would only be a "nothing" from the point of view of consciousness —which would tell us little more than we knew before.

The problem of dealing with the unconscious is, then, largely one of approach. The approach I have followed here lies within a broad historical framework that attempts to study the effects of the operation of the unconscious in creativity. From these effects the attempt is made to reconstruct the way the unconscious is formed and operates in the creative process.

THE IMAGINATION AND SENSUAL CREATIVITY

Probably one of the most difficult subjects in the whole of the philosophy of Immanuel Kant (1724-1804) is his doctrine of the imagination. As if the problem of the transcendental imagination in the *Critique of Pure Reason* were not difficult enough by itself, there is also, as he says, an aesthetic use of the imagination. But despite its difficulty the importance and depth of Kant's analysis, as well as its influence, can hardly be overestimated.

In his work entitled *Anthropology*, dealing with the philosophy of man, Kant briefly treats the question of the imagination in its relation to creativity. The word he uses, *Genie*, is a loaned word from the French; and he translates it by the German expression "eigentümlicher Geist," which might be put into English as "individual spirit." However, the German word *eigentümlich* with its basic root of *eigen* ("one's own") means that this "spirit" is not simply individual, but personally and peculiarly so.[1] Regarding the meaning of the word "spirit" (*Geist*), as used in this context, Kant observes in his *Critique of Judgment* that in an aesthetic sense the word refers to the stimulating principle of the mind.[2] Genius, he says, adds the element of "soul" or "spirit" to a speech, a poem, or a story, which might otherwise be dry, tedious, and without interest.

Kant insists that the right and proper area for the exercise of genius, the authentic realm of creativity, lies in the imagination (*Einbildungskraft*).[3] As a blind, but thoroughly indispensable function of the soul, we have no direct knowledge of the functioning of the imagination. We seldom, if ever, see it in operation, nor are we conscious of its functions.[4] Yet it is always at work; and the general idea of the imagination in its function is clear: it is a faculty that creates images in the absence of subjects.

In his various *Critiques*, representing the mature stage of his thought, Kant distinguishes between two kinds of imagination, the "productive" and the "reproductive." The *reproductive imagination* is subject to purely empirical laws, such as the laws of association, and thus, for Kant, falls under the province of psychology. This imagination, then, has nothing to do with what Kant calls "transcendental philosophy," that is, it is not concerned with the necessary, a priori conditions for the possibility of human knowledge in general. This latter is the function of the *productive imagination* which, as will be seen in greater detail, binds up the manifold of sensible intuition into a unity, thereby making our experience of an object of knowledge possible.[5]

However, making matters more difficult, Kant says that the productive imagination also has an "aesthetic" function that operates most powerfully in creativity (*Schaffung*). Indeed, the aesthetic side of the productive imagination, as Kant says in his *Critique of Judgment*, has a way of transforming the ordinary, everyday (*alltäglich*) world into something of interest. For in accordance with this aesthetic side of the productive imagination, experience itself can be reshuffled, transformed in terms of certain analogies and metaphors of experience, and this even at the higher levels of rational discourse.[6]

Thus Kant notes that the poet is able to "imagine" things for which there is not now, nor indeed could there be, an experience—at least so far as the poet is concerned. Thus, for example, the poet can write about death. Yet, death cannot possibly be an object of knowledge or experience. It could not possibly be experienced in the technical sense that Kant understands the word "experience." For at the very moment when such an experience might be "given," the poet would have ceased to experience, that is, he would cease being given "a given." Still, this idea of death is able to set in motion other intellectual ideas and related representations (*Nebenvorstellungen*), which enable the poet to write about it, even though this aesthetic idea, like a merely rational one, remains a concept to which no sensible intuition does or could directly correspond.

Even so, the aesthetic idea is able to broaden the whole base of the mind. Objects of knowledge, Kant insists, do have aesthetic attributes. And these aesthetic attributes are able to express a kinship (*Verwandtschaft*), a relationship with other ideas and concepts by exciting and stimulating the mind through the imagination, thus bringing into mental focus a whole host of related associations. It is in this sense that Kant referred to genius or to the creative spirit as the stimulating principle (*belebende Prinzip*) in the human mind. Indeed, there may actually be a concept appropriate to the aesthetic object that is produced in the imagination. Nevertheless, the rich and undeveloped material that comes along with the aesthetic idea contributes less to objective cognition than to a subjective enlivening, to a stimulation (*Belebung*) of the knowing powers in man.[7]

With this creativity of the aesthetic side of the productive imagination, Kant observes, man can become aware of his freedom from the purely psychological laws of association, even though a great deal of rich material may be drawn from this source. Even so, such material must be worked over (*verarbeitet*) into something entirely new and different, so that it clearly oversteps the bounds of nature.[8]

The intrinsic power of spontaneity that the imagination manifests, and hence the vision it gives of man's freedom from the merely empirical laws of association, provides a key for understanding the purely transcendental use of the imagination as it emerges within the argument of Kant's *Critique of Pure Reason*. Clearly both of these uses of the imagination are fundamentally productive. Both the aesthetic and the transcendental uses of the productive imagination involve an element of spontaneity. Nevertheless, there is also for Kant a fundamental difference between the two. The transcendental use of the imagination is subject to rules, namely, the rules of the categories or concepts of the understanding, whereas the aesthetic use of the imagination does not bring such rules into play. Thus in preparing or delivering a speech, for example, it is possible to arrange one's thoughts in two fundamentally different ways, that is, in an aesthetic manner (*modus aestheticus*) or in accordance with the categories (*modus logicus*). The former concentrates upon the feeling (*Gefühl*) of unity in the presentation; the latter, upon definite principles of logical development.[9] The spontaneity of the aesthetic use of the imagination is complete, whereas that of the transcendental imagination remains subject to the categories, namely, to the necessary, a priori rules of the understanding.

Upon turning to Kant's doctrine of the transcendental imagination in the first critique, one enters an area that is as difficult as it is fundamental to Kant's argument. Put most simply, it is in the transcendental imagination that unity is introduced into the sensory manifold. For Kant the undifferentiated manifold is pure receptivity. Any spontaneity possibly resulting from any such unification of the manifold could only proceed from the side of the understanding. All unity, any synthesis of the sensory manifold, derives ultimately from one source, namely, from the formidable sounding "transcendental unity of apperception," the "I think," which must accompany any and every representation. But since the *locus* for this necessary synthesis of the manifold of sensible intuition occurs in the transcendental imagination, this faculty becomes the central core to Kant's whole doctrine; for only in this way is the knowledge of a *particular* object of experience possible at all. This is the understanding's way of working (*Wirkung*) upon sensibility.[10] This is why Kant is able to say that the synthesis of the manifold through the imagination belongs to every piece of empirical knowledge.[11]

What has been said above may appear overly technical and unnecessarily complex, and the reader may wonder what is behind it all, or why Kant is being, as one might say, so difficult. And the answer is curiously a simple one: Kant is unwilling to accept sensation (in his terminology "inner sense") on face value. In order to answer the question "Why knowledge?" he must also consider the question "Why sensation?" However, as he suggested in his *Anthropology*, the German genius lies in its ability to get down to the roots (*Wurzel*) of things.[12] Kant is always looking for the transcendental mechanism behind things. He is interested in the necessary, a priori ground for there being an object of knowledge given at all in experience. Hence he cannot rest satisfied with accepting sensation as a simple and unquestionable "given." He feels he must get right down to the roots of sensation if he is to get down to the necessary and a priori conditions for the possibility of human knowing in general. And it is in this connection that Kant's doctrine of the transcendental imagination gains its fundamental importance.

Kant is convinced that there is more to perception, even to sensation, than simply the passive receptivity of impressions; there are images of *objects*. But in order for the image of *an* object to have been given, he reasons that there must first have been a synthesis of the sensory manifold, so that this knowledge of *an object* might be possible. Thus he states that every possible perception (*Wahrnehmung*) depends upon the primary synthesis of apprehension.[13]

In other words, what appears as the simple seeing of something (the sensible intuition) is not merely a matter of purely passive receptivity, a simple receiving of given impressions. Objects of empirical knowledge, he insists, are not vague impressions. There is always some particular object which is the object of experience.[14] This means that there must have been a differentiation within the sensory manifold already at the level of sense. Certainly the spontaneity necessary to effect such a synthesis of the sensory manifold could not have been brought about by the sensory manifold itself, since by definition this manifold is "manyfold." The unifying synthesis could only have come about through the transcendental imagination and under the categories. Only the categories could provide the unifying element to experience, and only the transcendental imagination could provide the absolutely necessary link between sense and understanding. It is for this reason that the so-called "figurative synthesis" or synthesis of apprehension represents for Kant a necessary part of the transcendental philosophy. The transcendental imagination, as he says, provides the unity of every manifold of intuition in inner sense.[15] The synthesis of apprehension, then, is to be considered part and parcel of Kant's transcendental philosophy, and thus also part and parcel of the possibility of human knowledge in general.

To many the synthesis of apprehension through the transcendental imagination may appear unnecessary. Why attempt to explain sensation? Is not sensation simply a given fact, which bears no "why?" But Kant has shown convincingly that it cannot be so simply considered. For even our sensation is not simply a mass of confused and undifferentiated impressions. If our knowledge is of *objects* of knowledge, then, Kant reasons, the raw material of the sensory manifold must already have undergone a synthesis such that it might be brought into mental focus.

This unifying of the sensory manifold, this bringing a determined intuition of an object into mental focus, occurs spontaneously. In fact, one might say that it occurs *unconsciously*, for man is not aware that this process of synthesis is taking place in the imagination. And yet it must have taken place. Kant will not be satisfied with accepting sensation as a mere fact, as a simple "given." Even sensation, vague as it may seem, is not without some definition. It has a definite pattern. And Kant would insist that this pattern represents a synthesis, which could only have come about through the unifying factor of the understanding. This would be the only possible source for such spontaneous action, since the reception of the sensory manifold as such would represent pure passivity. Thus if we actually do perceive what we sense, then Kant reasons that there must have been a synthesis of apprehension, even though unconscious.

It does not in any way surprise me that Kant should have chosen the same kind of imagination, namely, the productive, to describe both the unconscious workings of the synthesis of apprehension as well as the rationally stimulating "imaging" of the aesthetic use of the imagination. Both are, indeed, spontaneous, even though the aesthetic use of the imagination is even more free and spontaneous, since it works without any necessary reference to the rules or categories of the understanding. And like the reproductive imagination, as it operates under the laws of empirical psychology, the aesthetic use of the productive imagination makes abundant use of association.

In Kant we can in many ways recognize a perpetuation of one facet of the crisis of creativity, as it is mirrored in the phenomenon of the "two cultures," the roots of which we found already in Francis Bacon. As Kant says, creativity

(*Genie*) is a talent for art rather than for science (*Wissen-schaft*).[16] For since the aesthetic use of the productive imagination is not only spontaneous, but wholly free from any rules imposed upon it by the understanding, this means that creativity is permitted to have little or no place in the sciences. We can easily see the strait jacket into which science would be placed, were it to follow Kant's distinctions literally. Kant does not deny that creative genius is able to form all sorts of new ideas. Nevertheless, so far as any genuine and objective science is concerned, such ideas would be without value. These ideas depend primarily upon the admittedly rich, but nonetheless nontranscendental, association of ideas. And, as he insists, such association follows the laws of an empirical psychology, rather than those of transcendental philosophy concerned fundamentally with the establishment of the necessary and a priori conditions for scientific knowledge in general.

Kant's strictures against the use of empirical psychology may appear unnecessarily severe. However, we must always remember the sort of psychology he had in mind when he downgrades psychology and its empirically established laws. When he refers to empirical psychology, in contrast to transcendental philosophy, he is thinking primarily of the "psychologies" of John Locke and David Hume. For it is in this context that Kant criticizes the "famous Locke" and his attempt to establish a genealogy of metaphysical notions from common experience by means of some sort of physiology (*Physiologie*) of the human understanding.[17]

Certainly, however, such a criticism of empirical psychology cannot be interpreted as a critique of psychology, as it developed since the time of Locke and Hume and, particularly, during the nineteenth century, but rather as a part of Kant's critique against any attempt to establish the genesis of metaphysical notions solely by psychological means. In other words, it is very much to be doubted that if Kant were living today he would fail to make use of the resources and discoveries offered by modern psychology. He was not attacking empirical psychology as such, or as it existed in its barely viable infancy; he was attacking a psychology that was being made to carry more metaphysical weight than it could possibly carry—a psychology with metaphysical pretensions, but without the means necessary to consolidate such pretensions.

So far as he was concerned this psychology recognized laws for the association of ideas, but refused to go into the problem of the necessary origins for the very "ideas" that could be associated. In other words, Kant pointed out that there was more to sensation than meets the eye. He insisted that even in the apparently simple "given" of sensation there had to be a spontaneous synthesis proceeding from the understanding. It was true that there was no awareness of this synthesis; seldom, if ever, was it open to conscious inspection, as he says. In fact, we might argue that it had to be unconscious, and that it was a synthesis which could only be reconstructed.

However, we might carry Kant one step further, and by means of his thought throw an important light upon one of the necessary bases of creativity. For it may be argued that, insofar as this unification of the sensory manifold represents a synthesis which is productive of knowledge of an object, it is also to that extent creative, even though unconsciously so. In this sense Kant's choice of the expression "Transcendental Aesthetic," to describe the reception of the sensible intuition of an object given in space and time, would be a word well chosen. For it would tend to point up the creative character of human knowledge even at the level of sense.

For, we might ask, what exactly is the difference between noise and sound? And it might be answered that the difference is in a certain creativity at the level of sense. The ability of the human mind to create sound where a tone-deaf person may only hear noise would be an example of creativity on a purely sensual plane, just as the failure of the mind to create color in a person who is color-blind would represent the impossibility of creativity on this purely sensual plane.

In other words, sensual creativity would appear to be the most common and elemental form of creativity. But although it is elemental, it is far from elementary. In fact, it is probably one of the most complex forms of creativity to study in man. It has perennially resisted the attempts of scientists to determine the exact "how" whereby this most basic type of creativity actually works. Psychologists and physiologists have offered many explanations for this mysterious process of sensation in man, for example, in terms of physico-neural charges, chemico-physical impulses, dendrites and end-brushes, and so forth. However, far from satisfying us, these explanations bring us only to the point where sensual creativity of the type described actually does take place. As Kant pointed out, the process is essentially an unconscious one. We are not, nor could we be, conscious of the exact way that some tightly-drawn strands of horsetail, dragged across tightly-stretched cat gut, attached to a hollow, wooden sounding box could possibly produce in our ear the beautifully moving sound of a violin. We are conscious of the violinist and of his "sawing away" at his instrument. But of the process whereby the vibrations that his "sawing" produces are transformed into the beautiful melody in our mind's ear, of this we are unconscious. It is possible to reconstruct parts of the process, but it is impossible to describe it as a whole.

It is, of course, possible that the investigations carried on with certain types of computers, for example, the "Perceptron" as it is called, may succeed in throwing some light on this mysterious process. Generally, however, progress in developing or teaching computers how to "perceive" is hampered by our ignorance of analogous modes of perceptual knowledge in animals and in man. Try as we may, it is impossible to become conscious of sound waves striking the ear drum, nor are we able to make conscious the process whereby the physical and chemical impulses thus set into motion are transported from a particular region of sense to the brain. And we are not at all conscious of the process whereby those physico-chemical impulses, or whatever, are translated into sound. This last step is probably the most difficult of all. For example, there are persons who are tone-deaf. Apparently all the other steps in the process of sensation take place without difficulty except this last and most important one. The person who is tone-deaf picks up the same sound waves; the physico-chemical impulses are transported to the brain; and yet sound is not created. Indeed, if it were somehow possible to become conscious of this whole process whereby the sound waves set in motion by the violinist are translated into a beautiful melody—and if it were possible to analyze and study this process in all its intricate detail—would it not be possible, given certain scientific and technical advances, for the tone-deaf person to consult a specialist to have his musical ear rewired for sound?

However, the process in fact is and remains wholly unconscious. One reason why this is necessarily so lies in the very nature of sensation. Sensation is something that is always there, and this is possibly why it is so difficult to study. For to know what sensation is we should somehow have to know or experience what sensation is not—and somehow know what "nonsensation" is. And there is no time when we do not sense. Even when we are unconscious, or asleep, there is sensation, even though the level or degree of sensation might be minimal.[18]

In many ways, however, it is probably just as well that the process of sensual creativity is on the whole unconscious, at least from the point of view of our sanity. It would most likely be a horrible and frightening experience if we were, or could be, forced to experience the processes of sensation. The sensitivity needed to experience the process in all its detail would require an increase in sensitivity throughout the organism. And this could only lower the threshold of pain until we would also experience the processes of digestion, which would probably "feel" as bad as indigestion does now. Even then I am not sure that the critical point of sensual creativity, namely, the point at which noise becomes sound or the materials of sight become color, could be grasped within conscious experience.

I can think of one very good metaphysical reason why this process of sensual creativity will of necessity remain something that cannot be directly cognized, and this is because of the "psychic gap" between the body and the mind in man which must be jumped. In other words, sensual creativity, particularly of an aesthetic sort, falls between two poles, and as a result can be recognized by neither body nor mind. The organic side of the process is unconscious (and is possibly only "experienced" in sleep or in some other unconscious state), since by itself it is unable to leap the "psychic gap" to mind, even though its transformed and mutated content is able to do so; consequently, any study of sensual creativity is bound to be a difficult matter. It is only possible to reconstruct its operations in accordance with the way we think it must have occurred.

Difficult as it may be to analyze and study, however, it seems clear that sensual creativity plays an absolutely fundamental role in creativity of any sort, and for this reason we have treated it at the very start. It seems certain that the painter's sensitivity to color or the musician's sensitivity to sound has a physiological basis, and that this sensitivity is not unrelated to what we have termed "sensual creativity." The impressionist painter's sensitivity to the subtle pastels in a scene differed radically from the view of the same landscape by an academician of the same period. For the painter, it would seem, points out what he believes is worth seeing and being seen in the peculiar way that he actually sees it, as he attempts to portray that "seeing." And the reason why the artist actually does see more than does the ordinary man in the street must have a physical basis. When Wordsworth looked at a bed of daffodils, I suspect that it was due to his heightened sensitivity that he saw more *physically* than I would see by looking at the same bed of daffodils. In other words, the difference in the *way* that Wordsworth and the man in the street may look at the same bed of daffodils, the fact that Wordsworth sees much more, has a fundamentally physical basis.

This point can be exemplified in music. It is physical and physiological fact that different people have different aural limits at both ends of the sonic scale. For example, there is a limit below which a person will cease to hear a distinguishable tone, and hear only a vague, humming noise. Similarly, one person can ascend the musical scale to a point where the hearing of sound simply ceases, whereas another with a higher aural limit will continue to hear a distinct tone. This fact of the physical limits of sensation is not sufficiently emphasized in considerations of creativity. For we might argue that because of the very *physical* limits to sensual creativity in different people there will necessarily be varieties and degrees of sensitivity. And if it is correct to say that this physiological basis for sensitivity to sound forms the basis for sensitivity in music, then this will have repercussions at other levels of creativity in the individual person, whether in the appreciation, creative performance, or in the actual composition of music. Let us attempt to explain.

The ability to appreciate the various partials in the overtone series for a particular note, as scored for or played by a particular instrument, will certainly determine our appreciation of the music as a whole. And since each type of instrument possesses a different configuration in its overtone series, the sensitivity toward these overtones, which extends far beyond the keyboard of the piano, will determine what instrument an individual composer may orchestrate his melody for and the particular enjoyment which we may receive from listening to the music produced. Thus the composer who has within his aural memory the fullest possible spectrum of sound, the remembered richness of the overtone series of a melody played by the oboe in its various registers and performed by a particular oboist, will have a great advantage over a man whose musical "ear" does not ascend to such subtle reaches in the overtone series. The difference between a sensitive and mediocre performer, one may say, lies exactly in this—in the ability to sense and appreciate sensitively the full implications of musical tone.

This sensitivity with its fully physical basis is also shared by the painter. For the painter, much more than ever the ordinary man in the street, realizes the fuller implications of color. He realizes the artistic implications of placing one color next to this particular shade or hue, the blending and shading of this or that color into another, at root, because of his greater physiological sensitivity to colors. He realizes the full significance of different colors, and hence he can appreciate their nuances and variations in various combinations. Indeed, if an artist is asked why he chose this particular color and not another for this part of his painting, he will look puzzled or will declare the question ridiculous. Choosing this color and not another was for the painter automatic, almost unconscious, since it depended to a great extent upon the artist's sensitivity to the fuller range of the implications of color with its necessary basis in sensual creativity.

Indeed, there is more, much more to creativity in the arts than simply this creativity on a purely sensual level. Still, it seems clear that the sensitivity of the artist to sensations of a specific sort has a physical and physiological basis in the limits of sensation, which are both human and individual. It is no accident that many writers, and particularly artists and poets, tend to look upon their gifts as mysterious, and even as mystical. However, one of the sources for this mysterious power is as physical and prosaic as sensation. It appears at root mysterious because the very process of sensual creativity is "mysterious." It is unconscious in its workings, and yet fundamental in the formation of the overall sensitivity of the artist to beauty.

THE UNCONSCIOUS AND INSANITY

Certainly Sigmund Freud (1856-1939) was not the first to discover the unconscious. Freud himself acknowledges the strong influence which Schopenhauer's concept of "Will" exerted upon his own idea of the instinctual *libido*.[19]

However, there are other possible sources for the notion

of the unconscious. Thus, as we have seen earlier in this chapter, Kant insisted that the synthesis of apprehension, that is, the unification of the sensory manifold in accordance with the unity provided by the concepts of the understanding, so that there might be knowledge of *an object* of knowledge, was essentially unconscious in operation. There was no way this process could itself somehow be "imaged," and the reason why that process could not be given in consciousness lies in that it was adjudged by Kant to be the fundamental condition for there being anything "given" or "imaged" at all. In other words, for Kant, if there was sensation, then there had to be a prior and a necessary unification of the manifold in the sensible taking-in of experience of an object, and this occurred unconsciously.

Nevertheless, the idea of the unconscious was already contained implicitly in the doctrines of the Cartesians. Thus, for example, in his *Monadology* Leibnitz in his treatment of perception remarks that Descartes and his followers made a mistake in not taking into sufficient account the "perceptions" which one does not really perceive (*on ne s'apperçoit pas*).[20] The substance with a central monad or "entelechy" (namely, a soul, such as man) is never, according to Leibnitz, without perception; for this entelechy cannot persist or subsist without some affection, and this is its perception. Thus Leibnitz explains that when a tremendous number of these tiny perceptions (*petites perceptions*) occur, we are unable to distinguish satisfactorily between them and we become dizzy; and then we can distinguish nothing.[21]

This "awareness" of a perception which is not really perceived was, however, already implicit in Descartes and in his concept of "attention." Thus Descartes says that we only truly "see," or intuit, when we directly attend to something. This would imply there are perceptions and sensations that we do not really attend to, "perceptions" of which we are not actually aware, "perceptions" which we do not perceive.

Both Descartes and Leibnitz have made note of the fact that it is possible to pick things out (*distinguer*) or to fail to pick things out of a field of perception. It is possible to attend to certain items within a particular field of sensation by attending carefully to them or by failing to do so. They both insist that only in this way can we "perceive" those things that are perceived in the strict sense of that word.

And that which is thus picked out of a field of vision or sound corresponds, it seems to me, very closely to what Kant means by the unification of the sensory manifold on the part of the transcendental imagination through the unifying mediation of the categories or concepts of the understanding, which spontaneously and unconsciously introduces a unity into that manifold.

The point made by the Cartesians was certainly a valid one psychologically. It is perfectly true that what is picked out of a field of vision, or what we may be forced to pick out of a field of perception because of its attention-catching character, is always the fundamental point of departure for our conscious knowledge of a particular object of knowledge. This Kant saw, and expressed the idea even more clearly in terms of his transcendental philosophy.

Here, however, we are not concerned so much with the positive side as with the negative side of this idea. For it is clear that even those things that are not "seen" or "perceived" in the strict sense of these words, because they have not been immediately and directly attended to, also have a way of impinging themselves upon us. In fact, these sensations or "tiny perceptions" have a way of impressing themselves upon our faculties in a way which, because they are unconscious, may not be appreciated in their significance at the time. They can often be made subject to "recall" by means of drugs, hypnosis, or in dreams, which indicates that they were at least sensed. In other words, it is possible to recall something we did not know that we "knew"—something that was never for us, at least consciously, an object of knowledge.

Freud's discovery of the unconscious did not, of course, arise from extended studies of the philosophies of Descartes, Leibnitz, and Kant. He was principally a clinical psychologist, and thus he tended to develop his theories in psychology from his psychoanalytic practice and out of his studies of abnormal personality manifestations, along with heavy doses of classical Greek drama. But probably the most important element giving rise to his psychological theories on the nature and the role of the unconscious was his study and analysis of dreams. He saw in dream analysis a key for understanding the hidden impulses, drives, and anxieties behind overtly pathological personality manifestations that he encountered in his psychoanalytic practice.

According to Freudian theory the basic cause of neuroses lies in "frustration." These frustrations tend to arise in the following manner, as he explains in his "Thoughts on War and Death" (1915). Civilized society demands good conduct. This in turn demands the increasing suppression of instinct. And particularly in the area of sexual mores this enforced suppression of instinct results most readily in the "reaction-phenomena of neurotic disorders."[22]

In many ways Freud was as much an anthropologist as he was a psychologist or a psychiatrist. Thus from his studies in anthropology he found a striking similarity between the drives operating behind the social patterns and mores of primitive peoples and the repressed drives which manifested themselves in the mental disturbances of his

patients in the highly sophisticated society of late nine-
teenth- and early twentieth-century Vienna. The constant
and energetic suppression of such drives, and the frustration attendant upon such repression as they were manifested unconsciously in dreams or discovered through
hypnosis or drugs, could only lead, unless properly
channeled off, into reaction patterns which were or could
become neurotic.

The only salvation from such neurotic patterns of action
developing within the personality, according to Freud, lay
in channeling off these powerful and repressed impulses
into some external activity or other. Thus as he observes in
his "Contributions to the Psychology of Love" (1912),

> This very incapacity in the sexual instinct to yield full satis-
> faction as soon as it submits to the first demands of culture
> becomes the source, however, of the grandest cultural
> achievements, which are brought to birth by ever greater
> sublimation of the components of sexual instinct.[23]

The repression of sexual instinct imposed upon the individual by society can, then, become the source either for the
neurotic or the creative. There can be a sublimation of
the energy fomented by these instincts and by their energetic repression, so that these repressed instincts can be
channeled off into areas which are less harmful personally
and more acceptable socially.

It is in this way, then, that for Freud the unconscious
is related to creativity. The unconscious becomes the source
both for the creative and for the neurotic in man. It is the
source of the neurotic in man, in that the basic instinctual
urges are suppressed and withheld from becoming manifest
in keeping with the demands of society. The constant repression leads to an increasing pressure within the person

until he explodes in the blow-up of neurosis. But the unconscious is also the source for creativity as well. What might end up in neurosis in one could be creativity in another. The powerful and potentially dangerous repressed instincts can, by a sublimation of these repressed instincts, be channeled into creative, rather than in neurotic patterns of activity. Freud could not help but agree with the famous couplet of Dryden,

> Great Wits are sure to Madness near allied
> And thin Partitions do their Bounds divide.[24]

In fact, for Freud, if the artist or creative person did not allow an escape valve for his repressed instinctual urges into art, invention, or religion, the energy thus bottled up, and with no means of socially acceptable release, could only lead to the explosion of neurosis.

It must be admitted that in his published works Freud does not present a fully developed or fully consistent doctrine either of creativity or even of that element which is most central to his whole theory, namely, the unconscious. He was certainly correct in recognizing that only a small part of our knowledge is fully contained within consciousness. And he was able to adduce many phenomena to show that there was such a thing as an unconscious, and that it was much more than simply a necessary postulate for his theory of psychoanalysis. For example, there are "slips of the tongue" (*lapsus linguae*), which indicate an unconscious knowledge by association; there is the fact of dreams, and hence the possibility of dream analysis to reveal something of the repressed content of the unconscious; there is the phenomenon of posthypnotic suggestion; there is also the phenomenon Kant had referred to as "unconscious anxiety," pointing to a fear for which consciously known causes could not be produced; and finally, there is the fact of mental continuity being broken up by psychic events of great moment. In other words, Freud had a wide variety of psychic phenomena to which he might point in order to show both the existence and importance of the unconscious.

The unconscious could only be known through consciousness. Not that either consciousness or the unconscious were "things" which could somehow be localized exactly. They could be "localized" only to the extent that communication between the "two systems," namely, the system of the unconscious and that of consciousness, had to occur in order for psychoanalysis to achieve its desired effect. According to the psychoanalytic theory of Freud, the conscious idea had to overcome the resistance of the repressed unconscious idea, uniting itself with this unconscious "memory-trace." It would not be enough, according to Freud, simply to tell the patient what his trouble is; he must be made to *see* what his trouble is. That which had been thrust down deep into the unconscious, to all appearances irretrievably repressed, had somehow to be brought forth into the system of unconsciousness, so that the relationship between unconscious motivations and conscious facts might be fully seen. Another point of relation between the unconscious and consciousness in Freudian theory was what he called the "super-ego," a censor standing as a guard over the content of the unconscious mind, exercising its office at the point of transition between the two. That which arose from, or was firmly held within, the unconscious could become conscious only upon the prior "approval" of the censor.[25]

This communication between the two systems of conscious and the unconscious mind is not confined simply to repression, according to Freud; nor is it confined simply to the cure of the resulting neuroses through the seeing of the connection between unconscious reaction patterns and

conscious facts. Presumably, the sublimation of such repressed instincts into creativity of one sort or another would
point to an even more fruitful mode of communication
between consciousness and the unconscious.

In all this one must bear carefully in mind the social
milieu in which and against which Freud is writing. He
saw in the Victorian society of his day a social structure
which for both social and financial reasons did not permit
marriage until fairly late in life, long after the sexual drives
had reached their peak biologically. And since Victorian
society discountenanced extramarital sex, Freud saw in
the violent repression of such sexual urges, made necessary
by society, a fundamental cause of neurosis. Indeed, these
basic drives and repressed urges could be sublimated into
more socially acceptable channels of art, creativity, and
religion. Nevertheless, it is clear to see that Freud's theory
of neurosis represents a strong indictment of the social
mores of his age, as well as representing a theory of psychology. In the last analysis the blame for neurosis is
placed upon society itself. But by the same token one would
have to say that the "blame" for the creativity in the society
would derive from the same source.

Freud's theory of psychology, and hence also his related
theory of creativity, may, of course, be called into question
by his obviously one-sided approach to the problem of
neurosis. For even if the term *libido* is understood in its
broadest possible sense of a general pleasure instinct, there
are still neuroses which cannot be explained solely in terms
of the repression of this basic pleasure instinct. Similarly,
to say that creativity finds its necessary source in the
sublimation, in the channeling off of the energy produced
by the repression of such instincts, might serve to explain
art and religion in a Victorian society. But what about our

own? For in an age and society wherein greater permissiveness in the areas of *"libido"* exists, and people marry at an ever younger age, it would seem that in accordance with Freudian theory there should be correspondingly fewer cases of neurosis. But if there is less neurosis, then that should mean either that there is less repression of instinctual urges, or that there is a great deal more sublimation into areas of art and religion of the energy fomented through such repression.

Such does not, however, appear to be the case. Similarly, one may not accept uncritically the maxim that "Great Wits are sure to Madness near allied." Present-day psychologists tend to doubt that emotional illness or mental unbalance is either a necessary condition, or much less the actual cause for creativity. In fact, they tend to take exactly the opposite view. Creativity, whether in the artist or the scientist, represents the highest type of emotional health. Indeed, it is possible to point to artists, poets, and musicians who in their personal lives have exhibited marked manifestations of psychological disturbance. However, it would probably be best to say that their creative life was fruitful and productive *in spite of,* rather than *because of,* such psychological difficulties.

The Greeks recognized in the creativity of the artist a certain *mania.* However, this was less the madness of insanity than the "madness" of the inspired man. There is all the difference in the world between this kind of "madness" and that of the psychotic, between the reaction patterns of the creative person and those of the neurotic— which difference might best be characterized by the single word stereotype. The reaction patterns of the psychotic are inflexible, monotonous, and stereotyped. They are the exact opposite of the reaction patterns in the creative person, and they tend to make creativity of any real sort extremely difficult, if not impossible. Further, these fixed patterns of thought and action not only make it impossible for the psychotic to adapt to situations in a creative way, but also in time they render it impossible for him to adapt psychologically to *any* situation, even the most normal and apparently trivial. That which stands in his way is a fixed pattern of thought or behavior that is essentially uncreative in the rigidity of its response to any and every situation. The "Great Wits" of creativity are in no way to madness near allied. The problem of the psychotic is more fundamental; he is unable to adapt creatively, because, eventually, he is unable to adapt at all. The forms for possible adaptation have been fixed; his behavior is rigidly controlled by these fixed forms, making his response inflexible, his activity stereotyped. The psychotic thinks and acts in the same way in every situation. The patterns of action and thought that he develops have nothing to do with creativity.

At first sight, of course, it may appear as though the phantasies, hallucinations, and dreams of the psychotic are highly imaginative. But more often than not the thought patterns of the psychotic in their rigidity of function to any and every situation tend to become mechanical. Mechanistic in function, they tend to become so in structure as well. In any case, thought patterns which are mechanistic in structure and function would appear to be the very opposite of creativity, which appears always willing to discard old patterns and presuppositions to try new ones.

It is possibly on this score that Freud's explanation of many of the modern forms of psychosis is not so wide of the mark. Freud was very much aware of the elements of compulsion and frustration connected with psychoses. He attempted to localize the element of compulsion in the unconscious, that of frustration, arising from society. This would be true of everyone in society. But according to Freud the psychotic has repressed something from his conscious life, possibly a personally traumatic experience. In this repression he refuses to recognize this experience, his relation to it, or its relation to him. But this experience with its great personal moment for him requires more and more psychic energy in order to keep its personally unpleasant aspects repressed and out of conscious life. Thus greater energy is required to repress also those other incidents and experiences that are associated with this repressed fact or experience. And as more and more of one's conscious life becomes associated and connected, albeit unconsciously, with this repression, more and more of his time and energy becomes spent in withdrawing himself from the world of his conscious experience, until he is simply unable to adapt to the external world at all. He has systematically refused to recognize the pertinence of a particularly traumatic experience, and in so doing keeps withdrawing from the world of conscious existence while entering more deeply into an imaginary world of his own building.

This world that he has built up is not without method. In fact, it becomes a sort of mechanism or machine for dealing with the world or universe about him, and this tends to explain the mechanistic and stereotyped character of his responses to the external world which is not of his own building.

The physical model upon which Freud's theory of psychosis, and hence also his theory of creativity, would seem to be based is that of the steam engine. He would seem to have applied the key of the Industrial Revolution to the problem of explaining psychosis. The unconscious in

Freud's theory is like a large steam boiler. The more fuel that is added to the boiler system, that is, the greater the repression of instinctual urges, the greater will be the increase of pressure and temperature within the boiler. The scientific model Freud has chosen would appear to be Charles' Law for gases. The greater the repression the closer are the atoms and molecules of the gas in the boiler crowded together, so that there is an increase both in pressure and temperature within the container. But Freud provides an escape valve to this mechanism, namely, the sublimation of creativity, of art, or of religion. Without this escape valve only the explosion of psychosis would be the result.

It seems doubtful, however, that the necessity or urge to create can be explained simply as the necessary attempt on the part of the potentially psychotic to preserve mental stability. As psychologists increasingly recognize, creativity is not an escape vent for a sick mind, or simply the release of frustrated tendencies in man, so much as the full and complete actualization of man's deepest and richest potentialities. For creativity is not simply release; it is *patterned* release, as we shall see in the following chapters. And as such this patterned release could only come about by the full perfection of the capabilities of the individual to organize, pattern, and direct his creative responses to a wide variety of situations and possibilities.[26]

Freud is undoubtedly correct in pointing out the important role the unconscious plays in any process of creativity. However, to say that such creativity is merely a more socially acceptable form of neurosis seems unlikely. And even if creativity were nothing but a means of escaping psychosis, it would be impossible to determine. The unconscious is always something of which we are, by definition, unconscious. Freud himself noted that the unconscious can only be known through consciousness.[27] Nevertheless, the exact relationship between the unconscious and consciousness remains unclear in Freud's general theory. He looks upon them as two separate systems; however, there is obviously communication between the two systems. Things in the unconscious can become conscious; and experiences or events from conscious life can slip or be repressed into the unconscious.

The exact relationship between consciousness and the unconscious is by no means a simple one to delineate. The character of the difference is brought out in our language. We can say "I am conscious"; whereas it is impossible to say, "I am unconscious." And even after I have again regained consciousness, then it is still only possible to say, "I *was* unconscious." Nevertheless, even though it is not possible to say that "I *am* unconscious," it is possible to say that "I *have* an unconscious," even though, as Freud correctly pointed out, I can only make this statement because the unconscious has somehow become known through consciousnes. Indeed, it is exactly *because* man possesses a consciousness of himself, as a being that knows that *he* knows *what* he knows, that he is able to have an unconscious. This is simply to assert that man does not, indeed cannot *always* know that *he* knows and *what* he knows. In other words, man can forget both *what* he knows and even that he knows it. And it is this fact that gives the memory of man the peculiarly human meaning it possesses, and also its peculiar importance for creativity.

Nevertheless, although it is true that the unconscious can only be *known* through consciousness, it does not necessarily follow that the unconscious *exists* only against the background of consciousness. Rather it is the opposite. Consciousness, both in terms of the fact that I know and in terms of *what* I know, can only take place against the backdrop of the unconscious. This was something seen by Kant, and more expressly stated by Freud, namely, that there are mental processes which are unconscious in operation, and which, by necessity, precede any conscious reflection upon them or even conscious reflection upon the self that becomes aware of them. This might appear to make the self epiphenomenal, as in Hume: that the ego is simply the sum total of all its experiences and sensations. However, I think that upon closer examination it will only indicate that the ego is not given even to itself, independently of something that is given to it. The self can only reflect upon itself if it is first able to reflect upon its-self being given some-thing. I fail to see how there can possibly be self-reflection without reflection.

The fact that the unconscious can only become *known* through consciousness, and the correlative fact that consciousness can only *take place* against the background of the unconscious, assists in explaining how through hypnotism or through the use of certain drugs it is possible, even after a long lapse of time, to bring forth the "memory" of certain facts or experiences buried deep in the unconscious. But even more than this it explains how the sensations of things which we may not have consciously attended to at the time can also be "remembered," when we may not have thought that we knew them.

And it is here that the principal value of the unconscious for creativity lies, namely, as a vast storehouse of experiences that we received but never fully attended to at the time. This vast store of material can come forth or be brought forth to focus itself upon a particular problem at hand, along with the wealth of kindred associations the

unconscious may possess, producing a new insight or creative solution to that problem. Much of man's "knowledge"
is like this. It lies stored in the unconscious because it was
cast aside, momentarily forgotten, even consciously repressed, or simply because it was sensed but never consciously perceived in its individual detail. It all lies behind
the stage of consciousness, behind the backdrop of the
psychic unconscious, because the mind does not yet know
where it fits and why.

This is one of the reasons why the animal does not possess
an intelligence like that of man, much less the ability to
create. The animal does not *have* an unconscious; it *is*
unconscious. It has no awareness of the fact that it was
unconscious, because it does not possess the possibility of
becoming consciously aware that it was unconscious. Hence
it lacks both an intelligence like that of man, and the ability
to create. It is difficult for man to imagine what this would
be like, because he constantly has, or is at least able to
have, an awareness of himself as an individual. The type
of "consciousness" possessed by an animal might best be
compared to the sort of awareness man possesses when he
is asleep, with never the possibility of waking up.

THE IMPORTANCE OF FORGETTING

In his celebrated *Essay Concerning Human Understanding*
John Locke (1632-1704) speaks of the "tenacious, miracu-
lous instrument of the memory" as the "storehouse of our
ideas."[28] Nevertheless, following Thomas Hobbes in his
description of the imagination and the memory as "decay-
ing sense," Locke notes, "But yet there seems to be a con-

stant decay of all our ideas, even of those which are struck deepest. . . ." Thus it is that ". . . our minds represent to us those tombs to which we are approaching."[29]

Memory and forgetting remain an important part of human existence. And they are certainly not unrelated. As William James (1842-1910) observed in his *Principles of Psychology,* "The stream of thought flows on; but most of its segments fall into the bottomless abyss of oblivion."[30] Through memory we are able to recall events, experiences, impressions, facts, and so forth. And even those segments of our on-flowing conscious life that may have slipped to the bottom can be dredged up from beyond recall by means of drugs or hypnosis. They sometimes reappear in our dreams. But when events and experiences are "recalled" in this fashion, they do not represent the use of memory, since they are not necessarily rendered conscious to the individual. The use of the memory is, after all, the past made present, re-presented in *consciousness.*

This represents one of the more curious aspects of the relation between memory and forgetting, and one which will prove most important in understanding creativity. For in many ways forgetting is much more important for creativity than is remembering. In re-membering we put past events back together in consciousness. This sort of reconstruction is never as successful as we might like it to be.[31] All the witnesses to an accident may have seen the same accident, but with the passage of time, as more and more of the several segments of that experience slip into oblivion, the reconstruction of that event in the minds of the different witnesses at the time of a court trial reminds us of the fallibility of our memory and of the reconstruction of past events in consciousness. We must, of course, be very careful not to view this "constant decay of our ideas" either as an automatic or as an inexorable process, occurring at a constant velocity, as though there were an inverse proportion between the force and strength of a particular experience and the passage of time. As Locke points out, sometimes this "decay of all our ideas is willed, as well as being passive." Sometimes we *want* to forget; sometimes we do not want to forget, but forget anyway. In other words, forgetting does not simply represent a geometrically progressive dimming of an image or experience, or is it determined uniformly by the passage of time.

The element of time, then, has far less to do with remembering or forgetting than is ordinarily supposed. Thus James points out that forgetting is ". . . one instance of our mind's selective activity." Indeed, he observes, "If we remembered everything, we should on most occasions be as ill off as if we remembered nothing."[32] In many cases we actually wish to forget, even though we might not wish to admit this to ourselves. And it is often a blessing that we can and do forget. It would probably be more than the mind could bear, and we certainly would become ill if we had to remember all the unpleasant, painful, and possibly even terrifying personal and social experiences we have undergone. It is certainly a blessing that I can forget all about tipping over the bowl of gravy on the spotless white tablecloth of my host at a festive meal. Simply to recall the incident is to renew my feeling of embarrassment on that occasion. It is equally fortunate that the hostess on that occasion was able to forgive and forget the mess which I made of her prized tablecloth. We would both prefer to forget the whole incident. By forgetting all about it we can, in a way, pretend as though it never happened. It did,

of course, happen; and both the hostess and I still breathe
a sigh of silent relief when I have finished serving myself
with the gravy.

In such cases we actually *want* to forget. The incident
was unpleasant at the time, and its remembrance only
brings back a similar feeling of uneasiness. It is certainly
a blessing to our own peace of mind, as well as to our
relations with our fellow men, that we can and do forget.
Forgetting can, then, be selective. But it can also be haphazard, as James is careful to point out. For example, I may
meet an old friend or a fellow schoolmate whom I have not
seen in years; and for the life of me I cannot remember his
name. I certainly did not wish to forget his name, or at
least I do not think so. And yet, although I remember the
face, even though it has changed somewhat over the years,
still I cannot recall his name. I may even remember other
things about him, his present occupation, whom he married,
some shared experience; still the name escapes me. And
every pressure brought to bear upon my powers of recall
will not call forth the name. It is gone. I may be able to
pass off my ignorance in some more or less successful
manner, thus escaping from the socially embarrassing situation. And then, on the following day, possibly at some odd
and unexpected moment, the name all of a sudden comes
back to me. I knew it as well as I knew my own name.

The ability to forget is both selective and haphazard;
and so, it would seem, is the ability to remember. I may
fail to remember the name of my fellow schoolmate at the
time I need to remember it, and it comes back to me when
I have less need of it. And yet, I am able to pick out of my
memory the meaningless digits of my telephone number
spontaneously upon demand, without the slightest effort.

James points out that "As a rule, a man's memory is good

in the departments in which his interest is strong."[33] However, because of the peculiar relationship between memory and forgetting, I would suggest that this is just as true of man's ability to forget in his particular area of interest. And, as I shall try to show, it is as much our ability to forget as our ability to remember in the particular area of our interest that contributes to creativity. In other words, from the point of view of creativity in a particular area or field of study what we are able to forget may be even more important than what we are able to remember. Memory, we might almost say, is simply a less creative mode of forgetting. However, this somewhat paradoxical statement will require more explanation.

If we are correct in holding that the unconscious plays an extremely important part in the process of creativity, then, it would seem, the way in which different elements come to take up their place in the unconscious will be of paramount importance in understanding the way material for creativity comes to be organized. For it is by way of forgetting that a great deal of the material held in the unconscious comes to be there. As mentioned above, such forgetting can be either selective or haphazard. In other words, the way things are allowed to slip from consciousness can be both desirable and undesirable. It is desirable (even though it may not be consciously desired) to forget a particularly unpleasant experience or event. Such a forgetting may represent a deliberate nonattending. However, it may also be the result of an originally conscious and deliberate effort, in the nature of a "perceptual defense." Thus not only is it possible to forget what we may wish to forget, but also a "blocking mechanism" can be set up whereby a man may fail to perceive what he does not wish to perceive. In other words, the mechanism for selective forgetting in man can be made preselective, as in the case of the telegrapher who is able to pick his particular call numbers out of a scramble of coded signals and messages, while systematically forgetting to attend to everything else.

Our attention is naturally attracted toward a bright color, a catchy rhythm pattern, a loud noise, a strong smell, and so forth. We attend to them almost automatically. They excite our interest or repulsion, and we turn our head. However, because of man's ability at preselective forgetting, he can fail to attend to certain elements in a field of sensation, no matter how striking may be its detail. And it can occur that the person is not at all aware that this preselective ignoring is taking place. Such a person develops a psychological "blind spot." He has moved the process one step back from mere selective forgetting to a preselective perceiving. Not only does he find it easy to forget things that may be psychologically painful to him, but also may even fail to "see" them. He has set up a perceptual block against seeing what he may not wish to see. He may develop a certain type of "selective deafness," which is more psychological than physical, so that he fails to hear what he does not wish to hear. He may come to ignore the obvious. He need not even bother forgetting it; he did not see it or hear it in the first place. In fact, so far as he is concerned, it does not even exist; it has never existed at all.

That which makes all this possible is the unconscious. Without the unconscious there would be no forgetting, although it is conversely true that without forgetting there would be no content to the unconscious. In fact, without the unconscious and forgetting there would not even be remembering. For unless it is possible for things to slip from consciousness into the unconscious, there would be no reason for memory to attempt their recall.

What is the connection, however, between all this and creativity? It has been suggested earlier that forgetting is even more important to creativity than is remembering, that a man's ability to forget in his particular field of interest or endeavor is as important as his ability to remember. As James pointed out, man's memory tends to work best in the area of his particular interest. However, if memory is greatest here, so also is forgetting. For because of the peculiar relation between memory and forgetting, he is only able to remember what he has forgotten. With many matters, particularly with those in his particular area of interest, these "forgotten things" lie just below the surface of consciousness. They are easily recalled, easily connected and associated with the imaginations, facts, and experiences that are of special and immediate interest. In general, the memory is well organized. The facts and experiences remanded to human "memory banks" may have been so remanded for one very good reason: they will need to be used later. A person may need them sometime in the future and will often say, "I must remember that," and he may make a special effort or make use of some mnemonic device to help him do so. Or, associated with other material just below the level of consciousness, it may by itself be more easily recalled.

That things held in the memory somewhat below the level of consciousness are better organized can be understood, it seems, by the fact that matters not quite so well organized slip even more quickly from the possibility of conscious recall. Thus the nonsense syllables that may have been so laboriously memorized quickly slip into oblivion. They can be retained, even for long periods of time, but only with great energy or through the use of a mnemonic device. This is why, for example, musicians find it most difficult to memorize the musical scores of modern composers, rather than those of the classical masters. It is not simply because they have heard and played the classical scores more often. Rather, it is because, at least from a classical point of view, the modern scores seem less "organized"—the harmonies, rhythms, cadences, and so forth, are less what the performer is accustomed to hearing or expecting. By the same token, the student finds that the facts and information he has crammed into his head late at night, solely in order to pass an examination on the following day, are quickly lost once the exam is finished. For something to be retained in the memory it must somehow be related to the already organized memories. It is particularly for this reason that James is correct in saying that we tend to recall best those things that are connected with our own particular field of interest or study. This represents organized knowledge.

And those facts, experiences, or events that do not enter the memory in an organized fashion or are not able to be organized there in accordance with other and similar facts, experiences, and events easily slip further from consciousness. Their pertinence to the organic whole or human knowledge, both present, past, and even future, is not "seen," even if only unconsciously so.

We might imagine that this forgetting that cannot at the time be organized into man's present framework of knowledge would represent a serious drawback to creativity. In fact, exactly the opposite is true. The fact that man can "forgive and forget" is clearly a blessing not only from the viewpoint of mental health, or simply from the viewpoint of man's social intercourses with his fellow men, but also a blessing and a benefit for creativity as well. Being unable to forgive and forget, or refusing to do so, can lead to exactly that kind of single-minded, mechanical fixation common to many forms of neurosis and psychosis. For example, if a great deal of someone's time and mental energy is spent in dwelling upon some real or imagined slight to his person, a fixation can develop which warps the mind to the extent that he can think of nothing else. It begins to prey upon his mind. Being unable to forgive and forget is, then, fundamentally opposed to creativity, and closer to neurosis.

It might, indeed, be thought that the person with the best memory would be the most creative person; however, such is not necessarily the case. This is yet another reason why one must have certain doubts about the creative possibilities of Descartes' "method," which consists in the constant enumeration of elements until one "sees." It is as important to creativity to forget as it is to remember.

For example, being able to remember the telephone numbers and addresses of all the houses where I have lived could not necessarily be considered a creative use of my intelligence. In a sense Freud was entirely correct when he said that repression was necessary for creativity. He was not, I believe, correct in the way he meant it. For to be creative it is necessary actively to repress many of the nonessential things upon which one's mind is able to get "stuck." Certainly if the mind becomes fixed in its ways of thinking, held in its operations to a single, fixed idea, it can never move on to consider new matters and ideas with an open eye. There are times when ideas and particular modes of thought must be repressed or forgotten if the mind is to be freed for more important things.

This is, one may say, one of the problems with the electronic computers. Marvelous as the new electronic gadgets are in many respects, they suffer from one important drawback that must be overcome if they are ever in any way to approach the creativity of man. They must somehow be taught or programmed to "forgive and forget." The computers are amply equipped with memory banks; stored tapes provide further vast amounts of data and material at their disposal. Their "memories" are prodigious by human standards. They can "remember" a vast amount of facts and details, no matter how minute, reproduce them, and take all these into account in the "decisions" they make.

But the computers lack "forgetting banks." They are unable to forget a single one of these minute details, even the most irrelevant, many of which they should really ignore. The machines do, apparently, possess some means of "repression." However, such repression and forgetting are primarily organized and mechanical in character, and hence the machines do not achieve that sort of haphazard forgetting they would have to possess in order to approach the creativity characteristic of man. For if it is true that consciousness can take place only against the backdrop of the unconscious, and if it is a species of forgetting that builds up the unconscious, then it would appear that the development of a "computer consciousness" would depend most critically upon the construction of "forgetting banks," rather than upon the construction of more and more sophisticated memory banks.[34]

At the root of this difficulty to introduce into computers more and more of the traits of human intelligence is our very difficulty in understanding the analogous knowing processes in man. And at the root of this difficulty, again, lies the unconscious. The machines have something of an unconscious storing house in the memory banks. Analogously in man the material entering the memory must either enter organized or result in some unconscious organization, as we shall see when we come to association in the following chapter. But the forgetting that builds up the unconscious, and hence that which is one of the most important elements in the creative process although it can be selective, is more often than not haphazard and disorganized. This is why the unconscious world mirrored in our dreams tends to represent to us a fundamentally disorganized picture, a distorted world.

Such disorganized chaos contained within the unconscious is, however, something like the carbon molecule, to take a scientific model as an example. This is the molecule from which scientists generally feel that life derived and evolved. In the carbon molecule there is a loose association between the electrons, one which permits a wide variety of synthesis. The unconscious, it might be said, represents the same sort of chaos; it represents a loose association of experiences, images, psychic events, which can be linked together unconsciously in a wide variety of ways. Again, we experience these oftentimes odd linkings of experiences, psychic events, and so forth, in our sleep. And it is exactly the rich possibilities of such linkage—the linking of many of the disorganized and apparently forgotten images and experiences of conscious life in the unconscious—that play such an extremely important role in the life of creativity, just as the variety of linkages possible with the carbon molecule may have contributed to the origin and evolution of life.

Nevertheless, prior to any such unconscious linking there must be forgetting. And this represents the fundamental importance of forgetting for a creative use of the human mind. For any "reaching out beyond" to something new there must be a "letting go" of the old. Thus the mountain climber can only succeed in climbing the mountain, if he lets go of each one of his secure positions in its turn, reaching out beyond to a new one. Creativity is never "conservative" in the bad sense of that word. Certainly the creative person may be conservative, even very conservative in his dress or in his politics or in other areas of his private life. It is only in his particular field or area of special interest that he tends to prove very unconservative. The creative person is never completely satisfied with what he has done; or, at least, he does not remain self-satisfied for long. He is ever willing to attempt something new, to let go some of the apparently secure positions he may have reached, thus to "reach out beyond" to something new.

And in order thus to "let go," the person must learn to forget. This is, we might say, one of the fundamental tasks of education, namely, to teach students what it is important to forget. For if the student were to remember absolutely everything, if he were able to recall everything he has ever learned from every stage of his intellectual development, he could never become educated. He must forget some of what he has learned in any case, if only because what he often learns later tends to contradict what he has learned before. Education, particularly at its higher levels, is as much a process of unlearning as it is one of learning. The simple answers provided at earlier levels of instruction soon prove unsatisfactory, and must be set aside in favor of a more complete picture. And if the student refuses to "let go" what he has learned earlier, if he sticks doggedly by the knowledge of an earlier stage of his educational development, he can never hope to "reach out beyond" to the next stage of his educational development.

Nevertheless, the student can only learn what it is necessary to forget, if he is first of all able to know what is important to remember. The basis upon which things are remembered is not simply a question of time or of the dimming of images. Things are remembered because they are somehow considered essential or relevant. The more immediately relevant or essential different matters are judged to be, the closer they are kept just below the level of immediate consciousness and recall. And the other segments in the flow of conscious experience slip to the bottom of the river. They are forgotten. And it is good that they are. Such "irrelevant" details then cease to bother the mind; they cease to clutter up more immediate and immediately fruitful mental activity. Such things are put "out of mind," so that the mind may then proceed with more important and more pressing matters.

It is for this reason that systems of education depending largely upon rote memory fail to produce not simply creative minds, but even educated ones. The students in such systems are constantly being trained to "hold on" to data and material memorized (at least until after the examination), rather than trained to "let go," and to discriminate between what may and may not be "let go" in order to "reach out beyond." In other words, systems of education based upon rote memory do not teach the student how to think and how to choose between the important and the nonessential. And in this way the mind is left with the impossible task of remembering everything, which means that the haphazard forgetting that fills up the unconscious does not take place. The ability to forget is essentially more creative than the ability to remember. And this is why a system of education based upon rote memory fails to develop creative minds. It does not teach how to forget, since it fails to teach the means of determining what is and what is not important, by failing to train the ability to think and to choose intelligently.

In the chaos of the unconscious these forgotten and apparently irrelevant ideas and experiences, at least judged so at the time, are able to be held in readiness to come forth at odd and unexpected moments. For when things are forgotten, thrust down, or allowed to slip into the unconscious as irrelevant to the problem or study at hand, it is never possible to predict when they may again burst forth into consciousness. The reason for this lies in the simple fact that we do not remember that we have forgotten them. However, through the ever possible association of such "forgotten" psychic events and experiences, they may come forth from the unconscious. In other words, when they are forgotten, that is, when the mind saw no particular relevance to such ideas and experiences, it was impossible for the mind to determine whether or not, at some future time, such ideas might not be of paramount importance.

With the unconscious, then, man possesses an area of mind in which odd associations and haphazard syntheses are the order of the day. It contains experiences, ideas, and psychic events judged at one time as unimportant and nonessential, but which through a species of unconscious association, or separately, retain the possibility of coming to the fore of consciousness. And for the solution of a particular problem at hand such associations may be absolutely paramount.

This is the explanation, at least in part, for what are called *déjà vu* experiences: "I have been here before," though I am sure that I have not; "I have met this person somewhere before," and yet I am almost certain that such is not the case; or "I have had this conversation before," and yet I could not have. In the case of such experiences we have the weird impression of having "pre-experienced" something, which we are certain could not possibly have been experienced. In those experiences the mind seems to prepare itself unconsciously for something it "knows" that it will later experience consciously. And this preparation of experiencing occurs, I am convinced, through an unconscious joining of ideas and experiences, whether actual or possible, in the unconscious. It represents the ability of the unconscious mind to "visualize" through unconscious association a possibility of events that works faster than the actual "logic" of events. The same phenomenon can occur in dreams, as experience shows. The weird sensation accompanying the actual experience of something that has been "pre-experienced" in this fashion, derives exactly from this juxtaposition of the preconscious feeling with the appearance of the experience in consciousness.

This "unconscious thinking" is made possible by the forgetting that fills up the unconscious, particularly, we might say, in areas near or adjacent to our primary domain of interest or endeavor, whether this be in the arts or the sciences. In this sense Kant was certainly correct—man does synthesize independently of any immediately conscious activity. This occurs at the level of sensation, in the phenomenon we have described as "sensual creativity." However, it also occurs in the unconscious itself through the association of forgotten experiences and psychic events.

Nevertheless, even though such "unconscious thought," as it manifests itself in the distortions of our dreams, for example, does not represent a logically ordered process of thought; still such associations are not wholly random, or are they as haphazard as they might appear. For the forgetting that fills up the unconscious is not simply haphazard, it is also selective. Thus many of the elements that have been forgotten or ignored, or allowed to slip from the memory of possible conscious recall, may have been selec-

tively forgotten, deliberately ignored, or allowed to slip
from such conscious recall *for a reason*. This means that
many of the ideas, experiences or psychic events, which
have been forgotten or ignored because they are, at a particular time, considered irrelevant or unimportant, are
introduced into the unconscious for a specific reason. There
is, then, an order or pattern governing their entrance into
the unconscious and the positions they may take up therein.

This is, I believe, one of the necessary implications to
saying that forgetting is both selective and haphazard.
If it is selective, as well as haphazard, then this would account for the often patterned associations present in the
unconscious. Thus dreams are *something* like reality. And
the fact that our forgetting is haphazard also serves to
account for the fact that our dreams tend to represent
distortions of everyday experience. Not all our forgettings
enter into or form a pattern in the unconscious. The "thinking" which takes place in the unconscious, then, represents
a patterned and yet an unpatterned complex. It is a chaos
of the forgotten and the ignored, a chaos possessing its own
curious "logic." It is a logic of "feeling" rather than of fact,
a logic of intuition rather than of experience, a logic of
association rather than one of reason.

Certainly to deny the role and the importance of the unconscious in any assessment of human life, as well as its
place in creativity, would be impossible. For example, the
deep-rooted phenomena of prejudice and bias find their
basis much more in the "reason" and "logic" of the unconscious than in that of consciousness. This is why prejudice
is so difficult to root out of the mind. The "reasons" why it
is held are never discussed or brought up to the level of
consciousness, which means that they are seldom if ever
examined or reviewed. The deep-rooted, emotionally-based

prejudice becomes not unlike the fixation of the paranoic that someone is trying to kill him. The "reasons" for this belief are not rational, at least not in any conscious sense. And yet they are not absolutely irrational in the sense that they have not been carefully "thought out." The fixation has been unconsciously "thought out" and "reasoned to" through an association of every experience and idea around this one central unconscious feeling.

Thus the feeling of prejudice or of persecution is not wholly irrational; it has been "thought through." The problem arises from the way it has been "thought through," which is more unconscious than rationally conscious. This means that the actual reason the feeling is held to be true can seldom be brought to conscious awareness. This is why, as more and more of the experiences from daily life become associated in the unconscious with this central repressed "feeling" or experience, there become fewer and fewer safe topics for discussion and conscious thought until the psychotic or the extremely biased person comes to live most of his life in a world of his own unconscious creation.

Man is a curious being. Much of him remains hidden even to himself. We might say that the whole realm of the unconscious is nothing but the animal backdrop to the evolution of man. This certainly represents Freud's view of the unconscious in its relation to man. The unconscious is for Freud the kingdom wherein man's basic animal and instinctive urges hold sway and attempt to express themselves consciously. This is not, however, the whole story. It is perfectly true that consciousness in man can only take place against the backdrop of the unconscious. However, the peculiar sort of unconscious that man possesses exists only if there is a human consciousness. In other words, man's unconsciousness is able to contribute to creativity only because he possesses the sort of consciousness that he does, namely, one which is able to be aware of itself as a self. Only in this way is man able to forget in the haphazard and selective way that he does. Only for man is forgetting constitutive of an unconscious able to promote creativity.

THE ASSOCIATION OF IDEAS AND THE UNCONSCIOUS

To understand the importance of the unconscious for creativity we must also concern ourselves with the way ideas associate themselves in the unconscious. One of the ways whereby they do tend to associate, as we have seen in the preceding pages, is through the selective forgetting that introduces or finds patterned complexes within the unconscious.

The theory of the association of ideas is not something new in the history of Western thought. It can be traced far back into the history of Western philosophy. There are evidences, for example, both in Plato and in Aristotle. Thus in the *Phaedo*,[35] in connection with his doctrine of recollection, Plato insists upon the importance of similarity and difference in the association of sensible things with the ideas through recollection. Similarly Aristotle, in his work *On Memory*, notes that a series of thoughts may proceed from a present situation to other thoughts through similarity, contrast, or contiguity.[36] Aristotle thus even notes the ways in which ideas or thoughts may be associated.

However, it is primarily with the English empiricists, and particularly with Locke and Hume, that more fully worked out theories for the association of ideas begin to emerge. Locke, for instance, makes a distinction between ideas associated by "a *natural* correspondence," namely, that there is a visible agreement in the ideas themselves, and ideas associated by chance or according to custom.[37] Ideas become associated by custom in the sense that one can become "accustomed" to a particular melody, so that a certain note is associated with the one immediately preceding. Ideas can also become associated by chance; a feeling of unhappiness may be associated with a room in which a friend has died; a student may have a distaste for books because he was forced to read them in school. Hence Locke concludes that parents should watch ". . . carefully to prevent the undue connexion of ideas in the minds of young people."[38]

It is, however, with David Hume (1711-1776) that one encounters both a more complete as well as a more fundamental treatment of the association of ideas. It is more complete in that the philosopher attempts to reduce all association of ideas to three basic types. It is more fundamental in that Hume finds in the association of ideas not simply by the customary mode of man's reasoning about things, but also the way man's emotional and physical life is tied up with his mental activity and the material of such mental activity, namely, the ideas.

Hume begins by stating, curiously, that the ideas of the memory are stronger than those of the imagination. In the imagination the perception is "faint and languid."[39] This might be the reason why Hume can say that the order in the procession of images can more easily be changed, why such images can be mutated and combined, as in the production of winged horses and fiery dragons. The "fancy" or imagination is, after all, a very free faculty. However, Hume feels that the operation of the imagination in separation and reconstruction would be unaccountable except for certain "universal principles," from which the association of ideas actually arises. The principles for such associations of ideas are reduced by Hume to three: *resemblance*, whereby the mind moves from one idea to another resembling it; *contiguity* in time and place; and last but not least, the most extensive principle of association and the one which produces the "strongest connection in the fancy," namely, *cause and effect*.[40] By the connection of cause and effect Hume means that the appearance of the one in the imagination (for example, the cause) tends to introduce or call up the anticipation or expectation of the other (the effect).

For Hume, and this is more to our immediate purpose here, there is not simply an association of ideas but also an association of impressions. Impressions, he insists, are associated only by resemblance. Hence with joy are associated love, generosity, pride, and so forth.[41] The passions of various sorts are derived from the double relation of ideas and impressions. Thus the cause exciting the passion is related to the object, "which nature has attributed to the passion." And the sensation that the cause separately produces is related to the sensation of the passion.[42]

It is here that we approach more closely the sort of association of ideas as it emerges in modern psychology. Thus for Hume an idea is able to produce an impression, which when related to an impression connected with another idea, though related to that first idea by resemblance, is able to result in the inseparability of those two impressions, so that the one immediately calls up the other. It is in this manner, says Hume, that the causes of pride and humility are determined, so that if we were to remove pleasure and pain (the impressions whereby these passions are determined) there would be no pride or humility.[43]

Hume's observation of the easy connection which tends

to be made between ideas and their accompanying sensations is certainly a valid one. It may, indeed, be doubted that this is the sole way in which passions and emotions are triggered. Nevertheless, it does help to explain what might be called certain "emotionally toned" ideas. It explains, for example, the strong reaction that can be called forth by such ideas as "Communist" or "Fascist" in different circles. Thus when I call someone a "Communist," the designation is not a "pure" one. There is a whole train of strongly emotional associations which are called up, and which, almost automatically, accompany the application of the word.

But although Hume's original observation is a valid and valuable one for understanding such emotionally toned ideas, it seems to me that, for any understanding of the relation of the association to the unconscious and to creativity, he has the matter turned around. If I have understood him correctly, he says that, when an idea produces an impression, related to an impression connected with another idea related to the first, those impressions become inseparable, such that the one immediately calls up the other. This strikes me as curious. I should have thought that the association (possibly according to contiguity rather than resemblance) of the two impressions should have produced an inseparability of the *ideas*, rather than the ideas producing an inseparability of the impressions. For the inseparability of the two ideas would have been, so to speak, reinforced by the added emotional content of associated impressions or sensations. Thus if I am a Communist, the words "capitalist" and "imperialist" easily become connected because of the highly emotive connotations attached to these words through an emotionally toned propaganda.

Hume is, of course, primarily concerned with the reason why different ideas succeed one another. He attempts to formulate the "general principles" according to which one idea tends to call up others, and he finds the principles for the succession of associated ideas in resemblance, contiguity in space and time, cause and effect. However, I do not think that Hume has pushed his investigation far enough. He concerns himself with the reasons why different ideas tend to follow each other in a specific order, without ever explaining why there should be an association of ideas at all. Thus when he says that ideas tend to follow one another because there are resemblances between them, because they are contiguous in space and time, or because one customarily seems to follow upon the appearance of the other in the imagination, he has stated three "laws" for the succession of ideas, not the reason for the association of ideas.

Possibly one of the reasons why Hume fails at this point is because he fails to recognize the role of the unconscious. For him all such associations take place in the consciousness of the "fancy" or imagination. But, as he himself noted, there can occur a close connection between ideas and emotions. This is true, for example, in the case of bias and prejudice, in which the association, oftentimes unconscious, between emotions and ideas can produce a union which is difficult to "argue against" by any logical or conscious argument. And when those impressions and emotions are conjoined, the ideas that are so tightly related to them tend to become associated as well, only unconsciously. This is why the connection between the ideas cannot so easily be broken by conscious or reasoned argument; they have been associated not logically and consciously, but unconsciously through high toned emotions associated with them.

The way ideas tend to associate does not occur simply through their mutual association with sensations and impressions; there is also the association among ideas that have been forgotten. As has been pointed out earlier, forgetting can be either selective or haphazard. Those things selectively forgotten, as we have suggested, enter the unconscious in accordance with the "reason"—generally that of resemblance—why they are selectively forgotten. Those ideas, impressions, or experiences that are forgotten haphazardly do not enter the unconscious in any definite pattern; however, they can form a pattern by association through the similarity of sensations and impressions with which they are in turn associated. This is one of the sources for the odd and often unusual associations and the juxtaposing of different ideas that might not otherwise be associated or juxtaposed. The chief source for the association of such impressions, sensations, and emotions, and hence the accompanying association of ideas in the unconscious, from the particular area of one's concern lies in the element of passionate interest in everything associated with that particular discipline or area of interest. To the analysis of this all-important element of interest and its role in creativity we shall devote a separate chapter.

In many ways Hume explains the association of impressions or sensations far better than he explains the association of ideas. For him impressions or sensations are associated, as he says, only by resemblance,[44] whereas the association of the idea with its accompanying impression or sensation occurs in terms of the principle of cause and effect. Impressions and sensations, he says, become associated because of the resemblance of the ideas to which they are related. And it is this mutually interacting association of ideas and impressions that, according to Hume, produces the passions of humility and pride.

Hume might better have put the matter in exactly the opposite fashion. He might better have said that ideas become associated because the impressions or sensations connected with those ideas become conjoined, oftentimes for "reasons" of which we may be at the time unaware. In other words, the three reasons Hume offers for the association of ideas might better be used to explain the association of impressions and sensations. He would, I think, be more correct were he to say that it is for reasons of resemblance or contiguity in time or place (though not, possibly, of cause and effect) that certain impressions and sensations become associated and with them the ideas that accompany them.

The association of ideas, then, is not necessarily something haphazard and chaotic. It does not occur without reason or cause, even though the reasons or causes may appear as arbitrary as the joining of two impressions or sensations resembling each other or conjoined in space and time. And the fact that the passion and emotion associated with the particular field of one's interest and intensive study tends to associate all these sensations and impressions associated with it, means that the accompanying ideas, apparently haphazard in the way they enter and are associated in the unconscious, are able to form different but related patterns and relationships in the unconscious. In other words, even the imagined haphazard forgetting that occurs in the area of one's interest and study does not pass into an oblivion, never to be called up or never again able to be used. Just as selective forgetting is able to fill up the unconscious, and to form clusters of associated experiences and ideas, so also is the haphazard forgetting able to do the same. Following an insight provided by Hume, even the haphazard forgetting that occurs can associate with similar ideas and psychic events because of the related association with similar ideas and psychic events, and because of the association of sensations and impressions.

What does this sort of association of ideas in the unconscious have to do with creativity? In its root meaning the word association means to "unite," to "connect with" (*adsociare*). And it is because ideas can become united and connected with one another that a whole block of interconnected and unconsciously related ideas may break into consciousness as a whole. The reason for the novelty of such interconnected ideas and experiences is thus readily seen; the joining of the ideas has not occurred consciously, but unconsciously. And as they break into conscious experience, there is nothing of the element of familiarity about them. This would help to explain something of the great excitement that accompanies the emergence of such "new ideas" into consciousness. They appear to arise *ex nihilo*. They represent a new creation.

The way such ideas tend to emerge from their preparation in the unconscious mind through the various modes of association will be more fully examined in the following chapter. Let it only be said here that one of the chief mechanisms is that of *suggestion*. Again on this score we are indebted to Hume and his theory for the association of ideas. A particular experience or idea present in consciousness is able to suggest, to call forth from the unconscious other ideas, dimly remembered or even totally forgotten. Thus we tend to associate rosy cheeks with good health, so that when we observe a person with rosy cheeks the idea of good health is immediately suggested to us. This tends to occur automatically, and may even suggest itself unconsciously. Nevertheless, a different association might have been made. Thus rosy cheeks may suggest the idea of cold weather. Or we might tend to associate rosy cheeks with high blood pressure. Indeed, if our interest happened to be Tuscan painting from the eleventh to the thirteenth century, we might see in rosy cheeks an indication of a Byzantine influence upon pre-Renaissance painting in central Italy.

Such associations may be immediate and automatic. Our constant efforts and study in a particular area or discipline may make them even more so. One idea immediately suggests another, even a whole cluster of unconsciously conjoined ideas. This is why we may not be at all aware of the reasons behind particular associations that tend to be made. For those "reasons" are not necessarily consciously formed. There have been associations of sensations and impressions in our experience, which by being forgotten or ignored enter the unconscious to associate with other sensations and impressions unconsciously connected with them. These may have an importance later on, but it is not at all appreciated or realized at the time. And yet this association of impressions and sensations is able to produce a union of ideas which is extremely strong.

The sometimes odd associations often made are of particular interest to psychiatrists. Thus through word association tests, the clinical psychologist is able to discover some of the odd associations which the patient has made unconsciously, and which can thus indicate some of the unconscious "reasons" for a particular pathological state of mind. In such tests the psychiatrist reads a list of words, and the patient is asked to answer as quickly as possible with the word immediately suggested to him. The element of speed is important, since it will more likely represent a preconscious reaction, indicating the sort of associations unconsciously made.

Such unconsciously formed associations become extremely important in creativity as well. Oftentimes it is the odd and unusual associations a person makes that are of the greatest significance here. This is why something that might suggest itself to one person would not necessarily suggest itself to another. Each has different experiences and makes different associations from them. The associations made by the creative person—however "out of the ordinary" and "off-beat" they may appear, at least so far as the majority of his contemporaries are concerned—are in no way related to the rigid and fixed patterns of thought and behavior in the neurotic or psychotic. There is all the difference in the world between a healthy and an unhealthy mind. The associations made by the creative person are richly varied and vibrantly interesting. There is nothing of the tedious and stereotyped fixation such as is manifested in the thought and reaction patterns of the psychotic. In both cases the associations are unconsciously formed. But one fundamental difference is immediately apparent: the associations of the creative person are fruitful; those of the psychotic are not. Thus although the associations of the creative person may appear as unusual and "out of the ordinary" as those of the psychotic, they do not become fixed and rigid in their patterns. The associations of the psychotic are rigidly repetitive, whereas those of the creative person are marked by variety and versatility.

This represents another criticism that must be made of Hume's theory of association. According to Hume the so-called laws of association are based largely upon *custom*. Thus our belief that effect follows upon cause by an "infallible consequence" is founded solely in our customary belief that such will occur. He notes that de facto the impulse of one billiard ball upon another is attended by a motion of the second. Yet there is nothing in any particular instance of cause and effect to suggest the idea of a "necessary connection" between the two. Indeed, we are accustomed to associate the motion of the second billiard ball with that of the first; nevertheless, there is no "*inward* impression" of this.[45] The reason why they are associated in terms of cause and effect is that we are by custom customarily accustomed so to associate them.

This factor of custom bears closer examination. For if there is anything characteristic of the creative person, it is the fact that his associations, possibly *because* they are unconsciously made, are "uncustomary." They are not the sort of associations that a "normal" person customarily makes. The creative person does not associate the customary, nor does he associate that which people customarily associate. If anything, the associations made by the creative person are very uncustomary, unorthodox, and "out of the ordinary." Few, if any, had ever thought of looking at things precisely in that particular fashion before; few had made that particular connection.

There is also in the creative person a willingness to set aside the presuppositions and assumptions customarily made and ordinarily accepted. There is even a willingness to set aside cherished principles and assumptions which the individual creative person has himself long accepted as true, even when he may have been instrumental in establishing them in the first place. It is this willingness to "let go" of the firm and the secure and to strike out in a new direction that characterizes the mind of the creative person. This does not mean that he simply goes around rejecting the old, tearing apart old structures and ideas like an iconoclast, but that he uses the old to build the new.

Nevertheless, it is this basic and fundamental questioning of ordinarily accepted premises and assumptions that differentiates the investigations of the creative person from those of the uncreative. It is this same ability and willingness to overhaul the normally accepted structures of his own way of thinking that differentiates the creative person from the psychotic or the neurotic. In both cases the patterns of association are unusual; they are not the ones customarily made. But in the case of the psychotic those patterns become fixations that are essentially uncreative: first of all, because they tend to become rigid; secondly, because any questioning analysis of the presuppositions or assumptions for the pattern is not permitted.

In conclusion, then, it should be clear that the association of ideas, and the way such associations build up the unconscious, are of paramount importance for understanding creativity of any sort. For the unconscious is not simply built up by a selective forgetting or the preselective ignoring we have described above, but it is also built up through the apparently haphazard association of ideas that occurs through the connection such ideas have with connected sensations and impressions. Such association may appear haphazard, and this is undoubtedly the reason why the appearance of such unconsciously associated ideas seems so strange when they enter consciousness in their new connection.

James was essentially correct, I think, when he observed that man's memory is best in the areas of his interest. However, his forgetting is also best in this area. And when the element of interest—of passionate and involved dedication to a particular area or discipline—is also present, the association of ideas thus made possible in the unconscious through the conjunction of related experiences and impressions proves most advantageous to the building up of the unconscious. In this sense, then, the element of passionate involvement can be truly understood as the fundamental motivating force for the unconscious association of ideas

around a certain basic theme or pattern, which, because of
the higher emotional level achieved through this passionate
involvement, provides a veritable garden for the cross-pollination of ideas. It is this more than any other "emotion," as
will be explained shortly, that most strongly ministers to
the origin, growth, and fruition of creativity.

The Overflow of the Unconscious

In Book II of his *Ethics* Benedict Spinoza (1632-1677) concerns himself primarily with man's knowing faculty (*De
Mente*), at all its various levels. And in Proposition 50, the
first scholion, he discusses the origin and formation of such
"transcendental notions" as "being," "thing," and "something," as well as with the formation of what are termed
"abstract universals" such as "fruit" or "man."[46] Concerning
the origin of the former, Spinoza observes:

> The human body is able to form in a distinct manner
> (*distincte*) only a certain number of images . . . and if this
> number of images which the body is able to form distinctly
> be far exceeded, these images get all mixed up . . . the mind
> imagines every bodily thing in a confused manner and with-
> out any differentiation, comprehending them as though
> under one attribute, e.g., being, thing, etc.[47]

As Spinoza explains, transcendental notions come to be
formed in the imagination by a confusion of the highest
order (*summo gradu*). For him this is the case with the
abstract universals as well as with the transcendentals. The
philosopher is further convinced that this confusion of
images in the imagination is the chief cause for all the many
controversies in philosophy.

The images of things, as he explains, are simply ideas representing external bodies as though they were present.[48] It is thus, for example, that memory becomes a certain chain (*concatenatio*) of ideas, which chain is made according to the order of affections in the human body. Such a chain of ideas need not simply be physical; it can also be intellectual, as, for example, when the mind perceives something in a chain of reality through its first cause. However, it is through the chain of images in the memory that the mind is able to turn from one thing to the cognition of an idea which may be totally unrelated to the first. Thus a Roman might go along the links of a chain of ideas from apple (*pomum*) to the idea of fruit (*fructus*). This connection, he insists, is arranged in the body.[49] Spinoza does not make use of the word "association" to describe the formation and connection between ideas experienced in the body but preserved in a chain in the memory though he might certainly have done so.

However, as a result of the confusion of these ideas and images in the imagination, one can readily see how Spinoza finds ideas such as "man" or "thing" or "something" to be so confusing in their conceptions. In his view they could not possibly be formed in the same way (*eodem modo*) by all men. The variation would result both from the different things of the same type by which the body is so often affected, as well as from the mind, which is able to imagine and recollect one thing more easily than another.[50]

The formation of the transcendentals and abstract universals in Spinoza's thought is, I think, very similar to the way new and creative ideas tend to come forth into consciousness. He explains how the notion of "thing" (*Res*) comes to be formed in the imagination through the mind's perception in the body of things external to the body. These things that the mind thus perceives in the body represent many things. They all have one thing in common, however —they are things. The notion of "thing," then, becomes a sort of residue of confused experience centrifuged in the whirl of the imagination. It breaks into consciousness as the vague notion of "thing" which, obviously, can apply to almost any-thing. It is thus an idea or a notion without any differentiation or clarity. It is, after all, the result of a confused melee of experiences. It is for this reason, according to Spinoza, that all men possess a different idea of what a "thing" is. Because the notion lacks all positive differentiation, both individually and collectively, it could only be different for different people.

It is not surprising, then, that Spinoza looks upon such a confused and undifferentiated "association of ideas" as a very inferior level of knowledge—in fact, the lowest. Nevertheless, the philosopher is here describing a process, and one which can be very useful in understanding something of the creative process. For there are many similarities between the centrifuge process lying behind the formation of the idea of "thing" through a confusion of ideas in the imagination, according to Spinoza, and the process leading toward creativity that takes place in the unconscious.

Creativity of any sort is not a sudden affair. The solution to a particular problem, whether it be scientific or artistic, may appear quite suddenly and without immediately apparent causes. However, from what we have seen of the analysis of the role of forgetting and association of ideas in the unconscious, the apparent sudden flashes of immediate insight are not as sudden and unprepared as they may actually appear to conscious awareness. As many have noted and, I believe, correctly, the birth of a new idea in consciousness, not unlike the birth of a new offspring, requires a period of gestation. Hence, as D. A. Schon has correctly pointed out, the mechanistic explanations of creativity in terms of the association of ideas, whether in Hume or Spinoza, should not lead one to the false conclusion that creativity is a mechanical process or can be understood mechanistically.[51] Creativity, as Bergson would say, is not only like life; it is a way of life. The creative person is, like any living being, alive; and this is true of all the various operations and functions he may perform, whether conscious or unconscious. Thus the unconscious of man must never be understood as though it were a large electronic computer containing lifeless memory banks. The conscious mind, and the unconscious mind as well, is alive in its functions of selective and haphazard forgetting, in the patterned and apparently unpatterned association of ideas. The creative person is alive, and the process operating within him is alive as well. The gestation of creativity is a life within a life. It is assimilative and growing in the same way that the fetus lives and grows in the womb of its mother. And the assimilative association of new ideas through new experiences continually builds up the interconnected and interconnecting accumulation, which is the unconscious. This accumulation is not simply a chaotic mixture of atomic elements, after Freud's scientific model of a steam boiler about ready to blow up; rather, it is something building and growing organically, as does man himself.

Hence, the unconscious does not simply represent a chaos. Like anything alive there is an organizing process taking place in the unconscious. The process of organization is not, as we have attempted to show, ordered and patterned in the same way that man organizes and patterns his conscious life and thought. Yet, the order and pattern as they develop in the unconscious can emerge in a certain form in consciousness. And this emergence occurs through a certain overflow of the unconscious.

Upon first examination this unconscious overflow would seem to produce exactly the confusing lack of differentiation that Spinoza noted in regard to the formation of the abstract universals or transcendentals. And one might argue that this is what produces the necessity for the disciplined control of technique and craft in the arts, and for the careful observation and accurate experimentation in the sciences. For the unconscious is built up not simply through selective and haphazard forgetting or through the association of ideas connected with one's primary interest and work, but also by the personal and social experiences that are part and parcel of a man's life in the world. This point needs emphasis. It is perfectly true that one's forgetting is greatest in the area of one's interest, just as is memory. It is equally true that the association of ideas occurs most abundantly in conjunction with the passion of this dedicated interest in a particular field of labor and activity. Nevertheless, it remains equally true that the unconscious is also built up by the forgotten elements and associations making up our life of experience as men in a world.

This is certainly inevitable. No man can so compartmentalize his working life from the rest of his life to the extent that he lives in antiseptic intellectual surroundings which never feel the influence of his personal life and the life of the society wherein he lives. These personal and social elements in man's experience, then, also play an important part in the build-up of the unconscious. The artist or intellectual working in his ivory tower is largely a myth. Creativity does not, indeed cannot, take place within a cultural vacuum. It can only occur within a context, that is, within the context of the world in which a person lives and must live. For man is a living being living in a world—a world which is never entirely of his own creation, no matter how powerfully he may form it according to his ideas and dreams. And since creativity is a life within the life of a living man, this means that creativity must also take place within the context of a world which can only include the totality of a man's experience within that world.

This does not mean that a man's creativity will extend itself to all the areas of his experience. It is always primarily the area of his own interest, that to which he devotes his greater time and energy, which will most abundantly fill up the unconscious. Nevertheless, the influence of the personal and social aspects of his life upon his creative work is not without importance. When a person has been working on a particular problem or idea for some time—whether it be in the area of the arts or of science, in industry or in entertainment—most of his conscious working hours are absorbed with the study of his problem, with trying to work out his idea. With this continued absorption and concentration, as much is forgotten, or set aside as irrelevant, as is retained and utilized. Many of these elements of experience slip into the unconscious where they are able to be associated with other ideas and forgotten experiences. This association is not simply the joining of atoms and molecules into various idea compounds. All these disparate, but rejected, elements are assimilated into the unconscious to feed that life within a life. Along with these are assimilated the experiences of man's personal and social life within a world. In fact, it may be argued that it is the inclusion, however unconsciously made, of these various elements within the final solution and statement of the problem that to a great extent determines the social acceptance of many such new ideas and suggestions.

From this it would appear that the attempt to live one's life in certain airtight compartments does not necessarily promote creativity even in that area where one devotes most of one's time and energy. One's professional life constantly insinuates itself into one's private life, and man's private life can seldom be completely separated from his professional life. Indeed, it is very likely the cross-pollination of these two "lives" that produces many of the novel suggestions born from within the unconscious mind—often at odd moments from the wealth of assimilated associations between one's private and professional life. This is why the exclusive and single-minded concern with one's particular field of study, to the point of total neglect in the development and care of one's private and social life, may lead to a complete stultification of the spirit of creativity even within one's own field. In original ideas there is not simply the new and the unfamiliar, but also the old and familiar, the everyday elements of human experience arising more from the common personal and social experiences of a man, rather than simply from the dedicated involvement with a specialized area of interest.

Certainly this intimate connection between one's private and professional life, which is, at least in part, responsible for the fertility of man's creative mind, does not all take place within consciousness. In fact, while "on the job" one attempts in the best way to thrust aside personal or family problems as much as possible from what one is attempting to accomplish. These are matters that must be forgotten and ignored. They are pushed from consciousness by means of one's concentration upon the task at hand. And, thus, the unconscious association of these and other rejected pieces are associated and assimilated within the life of the unconscious.

This is one reason why creative ideas do not necessarily

coincide with the most intense periods of work within one's particular field of endeavor. A certain unconscious process of gestation may first be necessary. Indeed, the more conscious and intense the concentrated effort may be, the more blind one's insight into the solution of the problem. To miss the forest for the trees is an amusing metaphor, but also a very true one. All growth takes time; and this is no less true of the process of growth in the unconscious where ideas from the areas of one's active and unconscious interest become associated with those ideas and experiences from one's personal and social life that one has attempted to put out of mind during the actual period of labor. And this is why the creative ideas of the artist or the scientist's creative solutions to problems do not necessarily coincide with the artist's or scientist's most intense periods of work and thought. They take time to grow and develop, bursting forth into consciousness only when they are ripe, when they are viable.

This means that the exact moment for the emergence of a new idea into the fore of consciousness after the period of its unconscious preparation and process of gestation can never be predicted, much less completely controlled. This is one of the reasons for the loss of vitality in new ideas. They are able to burst forth into consciousness at odd and unexpected moments, and as a result the creative person may not always be able to take full advantage of them. By the same token, the composer may decide to sit down at his desk or piano at a particular hour with his composition paper, his writing instruments readily at hand, and nothing may be forthcoming. The creative life is a constant affair, and yet it is an inconstant affair. The very inconstancy of the fickle Muse that the artist seeks may be absent when he most desires her, present when he least expects her. Yet, it is a constant affair; so that even when the artist may feel

himself unable to work, he may yet be working. The unconscious process of gestation is working within him, and
will, if he is but patient, eventually come forth into consciousness. Like the expectant mother the artist expec-
tantly awaits a Muse who, he is sure, will eventually come.

The creative idea can, however, be lost. There occurs
here a phenomenon similar to that called the "after-image"
in psychology. Many bright ideas flash into the consciousness with the speed of lightning. And although lightning
may strike twice in the same place, it is seldom the same
lightning; for the unconscious has grown again in a new
and specialized fashion. The emergence of the bright, new
idea into consciousness, because it can occur so quickly
and unexpectedly, can just as quickly lose its brilliance.
And the remaining after-image may not possess the original
fullness and brilliance that its first flash represented. Thus
to get the whole of the new idea down in all the intricate
detail of its assimilated associations may not be easily accomplished.

On the other hand, however, this recording of all the
intricate detail of the assimilated associations may not even
be entirely desirable. It may be a monster that has entered
consciousness. And more often than not, the richly sugges-
tive associations born into consciousness are too raw and
crude in their original form. They must be refined, re-
formed, and reworked by technique and craft, if they are
to be presented most effectively, or even in an acceptable
form. Indeed, new ideas can lose something of their raw
creative force in this way; and there is no doubt that in the
arts, for example, an excessively sophisticated concern with
technique and craft can destroy much of the freshness and
originality of the new idea. Nevertheless, the submission
of the raw and unrefined ore from the unconscious to the
conscious refining powers of technique and intellectual,

artistic, or scientific discipline is also something not only inevitable, but also necessary. It is perfectly true that much can be lost; but much can also be gained in the effectiveness of expression, in the gifted reconstruction of the originally given idea from its after-image.

The raw power of the human imagination is, indeed, a marvel to behold! No power has so engaged man's curiosity as this one. For no power is so forceful in moving men's minds, in making the world over into the world of man's desires and his dreams, in remaking the elements of that world into objects of enjoyment and beauty. And the source for this awe-inspiring power of imagination which man possesses lies to a great extent in its originality upon the unconscious. It is no wonder that Freud could see in the unconscious the terrible and overpowering source both for creativity and for neurosis. For the power which both of these phenomena manifest, whether for personal or social good or ill, is indeed great. Through his ability to create, man is able to transform his world. He can create means of transport and media of communication that shrink his world in size; he can create a view of the physical universe through a simple formula, a few digits on a piece of paper; he can create works of art that transfigure his life, giving him pleasure and enjoyment; he can fashion a philosophical system that transforms the destinies of men and of nations.

SUMMARY AND CONCLUSION

Thus far we have attempted to investigate the role of the unconscious in the generative process of creativity. And because we are, by definition, unconscious of the unconscious, the only means which could be used to investigate the unconscious and its particular role in creativity were necessarily indirect ones. Thus we began with an analysis of creativity at the sensual level, a process of which man remains fundamentally unconscious, but, as we have seen, one that lies at the basis of sensitivity.

Because of the tremendous influence of Freud in any consideration of the unconscious and its workings, the relation of the unconscious to creativity on the one hand, and insanity on the other, had also to be considered. After that we concerned ourselves with the way the unconscious is built up. For if the unconscious plays a primary and fundamental role in the process of creativity, then the way the unconscious builds up, grows, and assimilates cannot be ignored. This led to a consideration of the relation between forgetting and the unconscious, as well as the problem of the association of ideas. Finally, the overflow of the unconscious into consciousness was treated in its relation to the creative process.

The fundamental problem in dealing with the unconscious is that of closing the gap between sensual creativity —the physically based sensitivity essentially unconscious in operation—and creativity on a higher and more conscious plane. We must close the gap between sensual creativity, as we have taken it from Kant, on the one hand, and the "quick wit" of Aristotle or the "intuition" of Descartes on the other. However, since consciousness can only take place against the backdrop of the unconscious—as we have argued—this means that any creativity at these higher levels of the human personality can only take place against the backdrop of the sensual creativity, which, even though it may be fundamentally unconscious in its workings, nevertheless provides the physical basis so necessary for creativity at any and every level, in any and every field of interest or endeavor.

For it is sensual creativity that is at the root of sensitivity. This physically based predisposition, particularly in the arts, ministers most strongly to creativity at the more conscious levels of human experience. This necessarily physical basis for sensitivity is, certainly in part, hereditary. Indeed, learning and education can sharpen these powers of sensitive receptivity. Thus the scientist, through training and experience in a particular area of science, can learn to perceive phenomena whose scientific importance may totally escape someone less prepared, less attuned, less "sensitized" by training and education to the reception and interpretation of such phenomena. Indeed, the physical basis of this sensitivity can be built upon; nevertheless, something must be present to build upon.

In other words, because the color-blind person lacks the sensual creativity of color, an almost insurmountable obstacle is placed in the way of his becoming a painter, with the sensitivity to the full implications of color which this necessarily demands. The lack of this sensual creativity in the area of color may mean a corresponding sharpening of sensitivity toward sound. Nevertheless, sensual creativity and thus the world of painting are largely closed to him.

The importance of this physical basis for sensitivity, and hence its importance for creativity as such, cannot be overemphasized. For upon this broad base does the whole of man's knowledge depend. All creative forgetting, the unconscious assimilation of ideas following upon an association of impressions and emotions—in fact, all of man's knowing is founded upon this basis. It is true that this process of sensual creativity is itself unconscious; nevertheless, the creativity at this most basic level is no less important for that reason.

5

The Climate of Creativity

One of the first, and very influential, works in the area of the psychology of creativity was a brief essay by the French mathematician Jules Henri Poincaré (1854-1912) entitled "Mathematical Creation," which was collected along with some of his other essays in a volume called *Science and Method*.[1]

One evening, faced with a difficult mathematical problem, and after much seemingly fruitless labor, Poincaré, contrary to custom, drank some black coffee. He could not sleep. As he says, "Ideas arose in crowds; I felt them collide until pairs interlocked, so to speak, making a stable combination."[2] Another stage of discovery came to him, he explains, as he was stepping into a bus. He was departing from his normal work schedule in order to make a trip. He adds, "I did not verify the idea . . . but I felt a perfect certainty."[3]

Later, occupied with a new, but not unrelated, question and having little success, Poincaré decided to take a trip to the seashore. He describes the result as, "One morning, walking on a bluff, the idea came to me, with just the same characteristics of brevity, suddenness and immediate certainty. . . ."[4] And one of the last pieces to the puzzle, he explains, fell into place as he was about to enter upon his military service. The actual formulation of the discovery he had made was not put into a final form until much later, after he had completed his military service.

THE ELEMENT OF INTEREST

From the genesis of this particular new idea in mathematics, Poincaré attempted to analyze some of the characteristics of creativity. He noted, first of all, the elements of brevity, of "sudden illumination," and of a "feeling of absolute certitude accompanying the inspiration."[5] Even beyond this Poincaré strongly emphasized the importance of what he called "unconscious work." Indeed, this unconscious work was both preceded and followed by conscious labor. Nevertheless, he saw in it the important function of providing a chaos, a disorder from which many possible combinations might be made.

Poincaré found another element in the unconscious, namely, a certain "unconscious freedom." As he says, "Invention is discernment, choice."[6] For in the consideration of a particular problem it may seem as though the possibilities of choice are infinite. And yet he found that in the actual process of creation nonuseful combinations are not made. Poincaré explains this choosing among useful combinations and the elimination of the useless ones as a manifestation of "unconscious freedom." He is convinced that the unconscious is not purely automatic in its operation. Choice and freedom operate also at the level of the unconscious. For in the workings of the unconscious, only useful combinations are made; or in any case only the useful and interesting combinations seem to break into consciousness.

And those that are "interesting" he understands as combinations which "take hold of our attention," because they possess a certain order, a certain harmony, even a certain beauty. Poincaré suggests that even the creativity of the mathematician and the physicist is driven on by an appreciation of the beautiful. For to the creative mathematician useful combinations are the most beautiful, and our attention is naturally drawn to them. The beautiful, useful combinations are the ones that break into consciousness—that "force" the choice of creativity.

As presented in this brief essay, Poincaré's theory of creativity, at least in mathematics, would seem to comprise several distinct phases or steps. There is the preliminary stage of conscious, but largely unsuccessful, working at the problem. This is followed by a period when the problem is thrust out of all conscious consideration, even though the "unconscious work" of combining and rejecting may continue. Then there occurs, often at an unexpected moment, a sudden flash of illumination, brief in its essential form but received with a feeling of complete certitude. Finally, the conscious work of the mind continues in the accurate synthesis and formulation of the solution to the problem.

Poincaré is certainly correct in his emphasis upon the element of choice in creativity, though I am convinced that the part which choice plays in creativity arises from a different source. He says there is an "unconscious choice," namely, the combining and rejecting powers of the unconscious, which forces only those combinations that are most useful and beautiful to break into consciousness. Nevertheless, this can, I think, be better explained in terms of the selective forgetting and haphazard association of ideas through their connection with related experiences and sensations.

Poincaré suggests that the reason for this "breaking into consciousness" is primarily aesthetic. The conscious mind is attracted naturally by the bright new idea, the truly beautiful and new combination of elements, and thus does it break forth into consciousness. In this he has underlined something psychologists have long recognized, namely, that there are attention-getting devices. These are able to excite almost automatically our conscious and attentive interest out of a field of sensation. And this is particularly the case when we are struck by the beauty of that which attracts our attention, whether that beauty be represented in a conscious sense experience or whether it arises from the unconscious. The beauty which is "attention-getting" is interesting. It excites our interest, and holds our attention. It is, indeed, this factor of *interest* which is essential for any understanding of creativity.

What exactly is interest? Taken back to its roots the word means "to be among" (*inter-esse*). Thus it came to mean in Latin "to live with" or "to take part in." Understood in its origins the word "interest" means to be right there in the middle of things. It is somewhat analogous to the "quick wit" (*agchinoia*) of Aristotle, the mind (*nous*) which is nearby (*agchi*), right there at the juncture of propositions in seeing the necessary connections.

However, the reason a person's interest or attention may be drawn to a particular new or original idea is not, I believe, simply a matter of aesthetic appearance. Not, indeed, that our attention is not drawn to the interesting or to the beautiful. Nevertheless, it is only so drawn because we ourselves are *interested,* that is, deeply and passionately involved in what we are doing. This is why our interest and attention are drawn to the interesting. The source of interest, then, is not attention; rather, the source of attention is interest. The interested subject is one who is among those things with which he is concerned, and intimately so. He not only takes part in the knowledge and discoveries made in his particular field or area of study as a disinterested bystander, but also, through the personal choice of his chosen vocation or profession, he has become personally and intimately involved. He is right there in the middle of it. He lives day and (sometimes) night with the problems connected with his particular field.

It is because a person has by choice made a particular field of endeavor or a particular vocation his own that he comes to be so deeply and personally involved in it. It is this personal, and even passionate, involvement in what he is doing that constitutes interest, and which also provides the emotional base for that association of ideas in the unconscious made at the level of sensation and experience, as we have attempted to show in the previous part.

In saying that the origin of interest lies in the choice of a particular field or vocation, only a part of the necessary climate for creativity has been indicated. For there are other conditions for the development of interest that must accompany the choice of a vocation which is creatively productive. The first and most obvious condition is, of course, ability. One may have a passionate desire to be a doctor; he may even have a deep personal interest in things medical; and yet, he may not possess the requisite ability to master the necessary studies.

There is another "ability" which conditions the interest generating a real call to a profession and that is, curiously, "nothing." The individual person must realize there is a "gap" in him that needs to be filled, that his life will never become anything truly worthwhile, whether to himself or to others, without the development of a passionate interest in and dedication to something. We often speak of "rebels in search of a cause." In a very real sense this is true of every man. Every man needs some cause to serve. He needs to dedicate his life and his efforts to something. He needs something to draw and absorb his interest, preferably something he considers worthwhile. Indeed, if a man does not have or develop interests, he dies. When he does nothing to fill that gap within him, that gap expands and he dies. It is the growth and fruition of interest which fills that gap within him. This "nothing," this gap within him which must be filled, is a part of that climate wherein creativity grows and takes shape. It is this "nothing" which assists in forcing the choice of a vocation or a profession which will fill that gap in his life. This is why a man must develop an interest in something. This is why if he has developed no interests, he dies. He may even die physically. Thus doctors will speak of men and women who have lost their "will to live"; they have lost all interest in living.

It is, then, normal and natural for man to develop interests; in fact, it is a necessity of existence. If a person fails to take a passionate interest in something, his personality can never develop fully; he can never truly become "integral." Integrity is simply "wholeness." And unless a man draws himself together—filling in the gaps within himself, which his ability makes possible—he can never fully develop as a man. There are many things that are able to draw man together, to integrate him with himself, and produce in him that deep and passionate interest which is *dedication*. Religion can do it, as can love; art can also do this, as can the persistent quest for knowledge and truth in whatever area or field he may choose.

But if interest and dedication are essential for life, they are even more essential for the life of creativity, the life within a life. They help to cultivate the rich and fertile field of the unconscious through the selective and haphazard forgetting which, along with the association of ideas, provides the abundant material for creativity in a particular art or science. For it is the passion of dedication that keeps one's mind and interest focused upon the problems constantly being faced by one working in a particular field of study. These problems exist in a field. They are not isolated, but interconnected one with the other. And as one lives with the particular problem for which he is attempting to find a solution, whether it be in the area of the arts or the sciences, he becomes intimately involved with all those factors and elements that are, or even might have some bearing upon, the solution to the problem at hand. As many of these factors and elements necessary for the solution to the problem are forgotten as are remembered. But the interest of the dedicated person working in this field, or context of work and study, provides an emotion and a passion which keep all the many disparate elements, some rejected or pushed down into the unconscious, somehow together.

The problem with which the *creative* person may be involved does not, however, create interest. Interest creates the problem as much as the problem creates interest. For a person must first *see* the problem before he can develop an interest sufficient to attempt its solution. It is not the problem that fulfills the need in man; rather, the problem makes man even more aware of the gap within himself and the need to fill it. Were it not for the passionate interest of dedication a man would "leave well-enough alone." It is far easier to bypass and to ignore problems than to tackle them head-on. And it is dedication that prompts a man to tackle those problems, rather than taking a line of lesser resistance.

Thus does a problem come to be through interest. And the passionate interest of dedication fills the gap in man; the problem merely calls attention to that gap, by drawing attention to the problem we ourselves are. For man himself is also a problem. In this sense Pope was quite right: "The proper study of Mankind is Man."

Interest, arising from the personal choice of a particular vocation or "call," originates problems, which in turn prompt man to seek their creative solution. These problems, in their turn, nourish interest. This is why the mind is drawn to the "interesting." It is drawn as surely as man himself is drawn into the necessary attempt to fill that gap within him, a gap more specifically revealed to him in his recognition of the problem. There are, of course, different ways in which this gap within man may be filled. It may be filled artificially by means of various distractions and escapes. Nevertheless, it can only be genuinely filled through the development of interest in some particular field of interest. This is the interest that will prompt a person to give to those problems he must face in the field of his chosen vocation that passion of dedication and involvement which will be creatively productive.

From this source alone, then, can true creativity emerge. For it is interest, arising from the recognition of problems in which men are and have chosen to be personally and intimately involved, that they find one of the necessary conditions for creative work in any field, whether in the arts or the sciences.

Some might see this element of "involvement" and of dedicated commitment as opposed to what is often called "the spirit of scientific objectivity." Indeed this may be so, although it would depend to a great extent upon what was meant by "scientific objectivity." Certainly the "creative" reading of a measuring gauge or an exact scientific instrument would be entirely out of place, no matter how committed or passionately involved a person might be with a certain pet theory he would like to see verified. Students will often do such "creative" interpretations of instruments and gauges in order to make the results of their experiments square with the textbook; however, this is neither creativity nor science.

In science there is a time and place for everything. The true scientist is always concerned with gaining the most accurate measurements possible and with recording his results with greatest care. This is the place for "scientific objectivity." Nevertheless, if the scientist never thought beyond that which could be immediately measured or presently observed, science would never have advanced to the point it has now reached. For science can only advance through projective thought, through projecting new ideas into the future for possible observations and experiment, while at the same time building upon the basic traditions of the science.

Poincaré recognized this necessary element of interest for any and all creative work when he observed that only those useful and beautiful combinations that are "interesting" tend to emanate from the unconscious. Nevertheless, they are worked upon in the unconscious only to the extent that they are struggled with for some period of time through conscious study and work. And the reason why these problems receive such exhaustive, and hence often exhausting, work and study must also find its basis in the element of interest. The problem may be seen only dimly at first, and it is the impulse of dedicated interest that prompts a man or a scientist to search it out in the first place.

However, if solutions to those problems come at moments

of leisure, at moments when the person may not actually be consciously involved with a problem, it is not as though these solutions arose out of nowhere or for no reason. They did not occur simply by accident, but rather at the end of a long, and more often than not, a tedious involvement with such problems, and questions related to them. And at the root of all this, again, he encounters the element of interest. For even the recognition that a new solution has been reached or a new idea gained would depend to a great extent upon his ability to accept that solution as the solution to the problem. And this in turn depends upon the interest that is nourished by a long and absorbed involvement with the data, questions, and approaches associated with the particular field of study and work, which in turn is the result of dedicated interest.

Creativity, then, generally belongs to a particular man reflectively working in the field of his primary interest. It is generally confined to that area within which the person spends most of his conscious working hours. This is one reason why creativity, as we have been discussing it here, has little or nothing to do with the way a man uses his leisure time. The hobbies which he may develop in his spare time are primarily "recreative," rather than creative. They are means of recreation and relaxation, something to take his mind off the tedious and monotonous tasks of the normal workaday world. And in this sense these hobbies can be eminently valuable even for a person's normal work, for they provide periods of escape and release. It is, indeed, possible to be creative even in a hobby; and there are certainly hobbies that are more or less creative. Nevertheless, our concern here is primarily with the creative, not with the recreative; and the relationship between hobbies, creative or otherwise, and creative work in a particular field is something very difficult to assess.

In recent years interdisciplinary groups, made up of members knowledgeable and creative in their own respective fields, have grown up, particularly for the purpose of solving problems in business and industry. In fact, this interdisciplinary approach to problems appears to be spreading into a wide variety of other professional areas as well. The benefit of bringing different minds together, each competent in his own particular area, each bringing his own particular talents and background to focus upon a particular problem, should be clear; and it may well become a pattern more and more common in the future. In fact, we may be approaching the end of that period of increasingly narrowing specialization which has so characterized professional and, hence, university life in recent years.

One such interdisciplinary group working for the solution of problems particularly in technology and industry, both for the invention and improvement of products, termed the new way it approaches problems "synectics." This program for discovery seems to base itself upon the liberal use of metaphors and analogies, or as one writer puts it, "the displacement of concepts."[7] However, they also make considerable use of "personifications," asking what may appear to be very curious questions, for example, "How would I feel if I were a spring?" "What would it feel like to be a piece of glass?"[8]

What might be the advantage toward creativity in asking such peculiar questions? Possibly the advantage may lie in the way such questions have of exciting and inspiring interest. The individual, in asking questions in this fashion and drawing others along with him, is of course quickly able to put himself, and others, "into the picture." Such persons are thus able to involve themselves immediately within the context or field where the problem they are attempting to solve lies. The problem can be grasped immediately "from the inside out," so to speak. For through the clever use of metaphors and personification, they are able to place themselves right there within it.

In a way this is exactly how a truly "creative" hunter or fisherman operates. He attempts to put himself in the place of the fish he is trying to hook; he attempts to take up a place in the world inhabited by the deer he is stalking. He must know what the deer or fish sees and hears, what sort of food they prefer, what their migrating and foraging habits may be, and so forth. The expert hunter or fisherman is something like Merlin the Magician in *The Tales of King Arthur,* who attempts to transform himself, as Merlin did Arthur, into different kinds of animals in order to know what the different animals saw and felt.

The romantic poet William Wordsworth (1770-1850), in his preface to the second edition (1800) of his *Lyrical Ballads,* described poetry as ". . . the spontaneous overflow of powerful feelings; it takes its origin from emotion recollected in tranquility." It might seem from this that the reactivation of a previously powerful emotion implies the attempt to gain a position of lessened involvement from that original powerful emotion. Nevertheless, it would be a grave mistake to conclude from this that the poet is seeking anything like the "critical objectivity" of the scientist, somehow placing himself at a safe distance from the strong and powerful emotion. The emotion remains strong and powerful. And it is exactly because of the deep and passionate involvement of the poet in his experiences that the reactivation of that emotion at some future date permits the production of great poetry. Thus the imagined "disengagement" of the romantic poet from the extremely powerful emotion is by no means complete; for even in tranquility that emotion is able to be reactivated, and with it the deeply personal feeling which it originally excited.

Not, indeed, that all poetry, much less all creativity, need follow this romantic model. Nevertheless, this element of deep and personal involvement, of sincere dedication to the area or field of one's specially chosen vocation, does represent a necessary condition for any sort of creativity in the arts and sciences. The conscious work one engages in is engaged in because of interest. The extremely hard work involved in creating a style in the arts depends upon one's passionate dedication and interest in doing so, just as the equally hard work involved in mastering the theory and techniques of a particular science also depends upon one's passionate interest and dedication. And, as we have attempted to show, the emotional basis for the unconscious association of ideas on and around a particular theme or problem also finds its basis in this passion of dedicated interest.

Who is Picasso, one might ask. He is a twentieth-century painter, we say. Indeed, he is a man like ourselves. Then what makes him different from us? And we should have to say that it is a combination of talent and a great deal of hard work. But why should he develop that talent through the hard work required in developing such a talent? And the answer to the question must lie in interest. We call him a painter because this is his profession, his vocation, his "call." It is to this that he has vowed and dedicated himself, his energies, and abilities.

The same is also true of the genuinely creative scientist. Certainly his work is the scientist's means of livelihood, just as Picasso's is painting. Nevertheless, his dedication and even devotion to his work, and the ability which he has developed to be creative in his field through this dedicated interest—these are things which cannot be purchased by an employer. Dedication is not a commodity sold openly in the marketplace. It is at a premium. It is, nevertheless, the most valuable "commodity" an employer can obtain. And though it can be fostered and encouraged, it cannot be bought and sold.

It is often said that there is no such thing as an uncreative child. Their fresh ways of thinking and of looking at things, the confounding originality of their questions, even the simple ingenuity of their play—all these things may prompt the astonished adult to believe that children are essentially creative. What happens, some ask, to this raw creative energy in children. What makes it disappear in later years? Was it wrongly channeled? Or is it lost in the crash of adolescent idealism?

First of all, I have very serious doubts about the so-called creativity of children. It is true that the child has a freshness, a "wonder" which may be the envy of a cynical, adult mind. Nevertheless, there is one thing the child lacks that is at the basis of the productive wonder of the creative artist or scientist, and that is the element of interest and passionate dedication. Indeed, the child asks "Why?" "What's this?" "Why is that so?" And yet the parent who is patient enough to answer all such questions in their turn soon finds that almost any answer will satisfy the child.

The wonderfully fresh originality of children's questions is, I think, deceptive. More often than not the child does not even wait for the answer. Something else interests him. But nothing interests him with the passionate dedication characteristic of the creative person. In fact, the child appears to ask questions simply for the sake of asking questions. He may ask them in the delirious joy of his new discovery, the magic of language. He may ask them in order to make sure that his parents love him enough to give him the answers he is absolutely certain they possess. Or he may ask them to make sure that there are answers to his questions. He does not care what answers, just answers. In fact, one question is barely answered, or hardly answered at all; and another, often in no way related, follows immediately upon the heels of the first.

What is lacking here is the passionate interest of dedication—the lack that is at the root of the child's failure to see the problems involved in the questions he asks. The questions the child asks are not, however, related to anything more fundamental than the question which is being asked. This is why almost any answer will be accepted as satisfactory. The child does not see the problem, something he would see only if his passionate interest in the questions he asked were grounded in the realization of the gap he must fill. It is because the child does not see the problem that almost any answer will suffice. This is also the reason why he will often not even wait for the answer.

This is also why one of the greatest problems in education is that of making the student see the problems. Only in this way can his interest in his education be furthered. For if the student fails to see the problems, answers given to questions become separated abstractly from the whole reason for asking the questions in the first place. And certainly when the educational process degenerates into a mere supplying of answers to the student—these to be repeated by the student for the examination—genuine learning is simply obviated, and the opportunity for the development of creative thought lost.

The child's imaginative play, the often profound questions he may ask, the freshness and freedom of his art work in school—all these things may lead the adult to believe that children are fundamentally creative; and, therefore, that creativity in adults can best be fostered by taking the outlook of the child. Such could not be further from the truth. The adult possesses something the child does not, the passionate interest of dedication. It is entirely true that children can become deeply engrossed in their play. There is the little toy car with a whole world of imagined roads and other cars and people. The child's imagination is so strong that it requires precious little to create a whole world of play. A simple block of wood or a stone can symbolize a bulldozer or a road grader. Yet, engrossed as he may be in his play—so engrossed that he may fail to hear his mother's insistent calls—the child is not really passionately involved in his game. He can throw down one game and pick up another most readily, without feeling any remorse for failing to complete or "solve" the first one, in the same way that he can drop one question and pick up another without ever having received an answer to his first question. In his eternal questioning the child has not yet become personally and passionately involved in the questions he asks. He may become engrossed, but he has not yet developed that magic motive force of interest, the passionate dedication of a vocation to truth or beauty which enables a man, first of all, to see; and, secondly, to seek passionately the solution of problems.

I would not, of course, wish to downgrade the importance of the aimless and apparently purposeless activity of play in children. For I am equally convinced that it is by means of the development of the imagination through the phantasies and day-dreams of child's play that provides most powerfully for the growth and development of the creative mind in later life. The apparently purposeless activity of play is an essential and integral part of the child's formation and growth. This is the reason why many psychologists and sociologists are rightly disturbed by the shortening of this period of "latency" or of childhood play; they are disturbed that children are forced to enter a world of adult competition even earlier in life.

Nonetheless, from what has been said above, it should not be concluded that the particular way the theoretical physicist may "play" with different solutions to the puzzle of the universe is simply a more advanced form of "child's play." Again, there is all the difference in the world between the sometimes painfully serious play the scientist indulges in and the play of the child. Each time the scientist performs an experiment, he is laying his theory on the line, and the possible failure of the experiment—and with it his theory—will mean an agonizing reappraisal of the basic assumptions and presuppositions he made and of which he was so certain. The child does not possess the requisite stamina of mind necessary to indulge in this sort of "play," and the reason why he does not possess it is because he has not yet developed that interest of passionate dedication to truth or beauty which the true scientist or artist possesses.

It is this element of interest and of passionate dedication that must somehow be introduced into the computers if they are ever to be made "creative." In other words, in addition to the "forgetting banks" the fashioners of computers must somehow figure out a way to introduce "love" and "passion" into the machines they make. The computers must somehow be made to desire the truth with a passion. Only in this way can the unconscious association of ideas arising from the emotion of dedicated interest be accomplished. As Aristotle notes in the opening line of his *Meta-physics*, "All men by the very nature which is theirs *desire* to know." It is this passionate desire that the designers of computers must somehow instill into the machines. Whether love and passionate dedication can be simulated mechanically, I do not claim to know. Nevertheless, it is these peculiarly human traits of love and dedication that stand behind the passion of creativity, a passion which generates the creative life within a life.

Chaos and Life

In many ways the father of most modern theories of creativity is the French thinker Henri Bergson (1859-1941). And it is, in a way, natural that many of these theories of creativity should draw much of their inspiration from a man who, all his life, fought against the machine.

Not, of course, that Bergson opposed the rapid techno-logical advances of science in the invention and utilization of material instruments used to gain control over nature. His attack against the modern technological age was both more subtle, as well as more fundamental. He denied, and did his best to subvert, the basic scientific view of the universe from Newton down to his own day, which scientific view he saw as essentially mechanistic. In other words, Bergson was not so much against the machines, as against viewing the whole universe as one vast machine.

It was in this spirit, for example, that Bergson criticized "entropy" as essentially a mechanistic law. Entropy, as it derives from the second law of thermodynamics in physics, states that once energy has been extracted from a system, less energy can be extracted from that same source in the future. This does not mean that the energy has disappeared. It is still around, but it can be regained and reused only through the expending of a much greater amount of energy. The increase in entropy is seen as a necessarily downhill process. For as the amount of available energy becomes more and more diffused throughout the universe, until that energy becomes equally diffused throughout, there results what is called a "heat death." This is the situation in which the universe would attain the same uniform level of temperature, namely, all the *available* energy in the universe would have been used up. This tendency of energy toward a uniform level of diffusion is interpreted by some scientists as a tendency toward disorder.

Bergson was aware of this conclusion drawn from the second law of thermodynamics. But, in the first place, he was convinced that the law was fundamentally undemonstrable. Secondly, he insisted that even as there might be worlds which would die from this process of energy diffusion, because of the loss of all available energy—in other words, even as there are worlds which are dying—so also are there worlds which are constantly being born. And this would be particularly true in a world of living things.[9]

Bergson's criticism was a just one. It is, indeed, entirely true that increasing entropy is fundamentally a downhill process. Nevertheless, this process of devolution is reversed by living things. Thus in terms of the law of entropy one would have to say that a growing plant is able to "consume" entropy, that is, reverse the process toward every increasing entropy in the world. Thus the plant is able to take the random and diffused molecules of oxygen, hydrogen, carbon, and nitrogen out of the air, water, and soil, and arrange them in accordance with the structured function that is life. A living organism is able to organize all these disparate elements into itself, to assimilate them into the process we call living. It is in this sense that life may be said to be "creative"; in a physical universe of increasing entropy living organisms are able to form little islands of decreasing, of consuming, entropy.

Modern evolutionary theory tends to explain the origin of life in essentially the same fashion. The ordered structure-function which represents life arose out of a primordial chaos and disorder. Life, it is said, arose out of the medium of water in which were contained the huge unmanageable carbon chains with their loose valence bonds, and hence with their broad possibilities for synthesis. In the chaos of these huge and unwieldy chains of loosely-connected molecules there was a basic instability. This instability toward entropy-increasing diffusion or toward even more unwieldy and unstable carbon chains could only be held together through an internal ordering and reordering process which we understand as life—in other words, life developed as a necessary inner-organizing force to keep things together. As Bergson put it, evolution is in the direction of individuality and association.[10]

The next stage in the development of modern theories of creativity was easily reached. Bergson had already prepared the way. He had already insisted that consciousness, which he had described as a fundamental and necessary tendency of creation (*exigence de création*), only manifests itself to itself where its creation is possible.[11] By this he means, as he explains a little later, that human consciousness is somehow "preformed" (*préformée*) in the evolutionary movement which leads, of necessity, up to man.[12] Consciousness, Bergson feels, was a necessary culmination to the process of evolutionary development. This means, however, that an elemental form of the creativity of consciousness must already have been there as an evolutionary possibility from the very beginning of evolution. This tends to give Bergson's explanation of the evolutionary *élan vital* a very broad form of continuity. It also indicates how the creativity of consciousness was and had to be contained within the creative, changing, evolving flow of reality as its ultimate possibility.[13]

It is because the creative consciousness of man is already "pre-formed," and because it is already necessarily implicit in the whole process whereby consciousness comes to cap this long process of evolution, that Bergson is able to move to the next step in his reasoning. For since consciousness is somehow already contained in embryo, so to speak, within the whole evolutionary process, then this means that if man wishes to "get into the knowledge" of this ever-changing, ever-evolving universe, then a very special kind of knowledge, one which is vibrantly attuned to this ever-changing, ever-evolving universe, must be employed. And Bergson calls this primary creative function of the knowing mind, which truly "gets with" the evolving, changing flow of things, *intuition*. It is this power, which has grown out of that very process of evolution that is best able to get back into that flow and to grasp it in its inner reality.

Certainly intuition does not mean here what it meant for Descartes. The world of Descartes is a mechanistic one; that of Bergson, a living, evolutionary one. This power of intuition in Bergson is like the inner, changing, living reality which it intuits. In other words, this intuition is far from the lifeless, dead faculty of Descartes; rather, it is vibrantly alive. Intuition is, as Bergson observes, in a certain sense life itself.[14] And hence this power intuiting directly into the heart of a living, flowing reality is always there, even when it is not used. Since it is at the end point of the long and richly superabundant process of evolution, capping that process, it is able to intuit that reality in its inherent process.

One can easily see how Bergson's ideas on intuition and evolution can set the stage for many modern theories of creativity, particularly those that understood creativity as somehow an intuition into the truth of things. For Bergson creativity is a life. It is a way of life that is as creative as life itself. And what is life? Life is that which brings order out of a chaos. Thus just as an organism is able to organize a chaos of organic matter into an order—the living order that living thing must become in order to be—so also does the creative person, for example in the physical sciences, organize the chaos of many facts, experimental data, theories, and observations into an order, a scientific formula.

This belief that creativity arises out of a primordial disorder derives from sources other than a theoretical consideration of the nature of life. Thus some writers on creativity point to the cluttered and disordered studios and workshops of artists. It is imagined that this very disorder in the surroundings where the artist works has some relation to the creativity of the artist. For if creativity represents an ordering of the disordered, then the reason for the cluttered studios of artists is more readily explained.

Similarly, there are those psychologists who have more recently pointed out that the creative person tends to think in less symmetrical patterns than does the less creative, though possibly more intelligent, person. Thus through the establishment of various tests psychologists have devised means of determining the characteristics of what they describe as the "intelligent" person, as contrasted with the "creative" person. Persons with high intelligence are found to have very "symmetrical" minds; they are orderly in their processes of thinking and in the way they have of looking at things; whereas those who are more creative are found to possess "asymmetrical" minds, minds which look at things in different and even in odd fashions.

In many ways this distinction between intelligence and creativity had already been drawn by Bergson. For him intelligence was the field of the practical man. Thus in his view the creative person could always become an intelligent one; but from intelligence one could never pass over to intuition,[15] namely, to creativity.

It is true that many people had seen beds of daffodils before Wordsworth. Hence, it must lie in the peculiar and asymmetrical way in which Wordsworth looked at that bed of daffodils that made it possible for him to create his poem. But since the creative person tends to see things in peculiar and asymmetrical ways, it can be understood why creativity has come to be associated with the eccentric and the odd. It may be for this reason that pseudo artists feel obliged to strike an artistic pose by appearing odd, eccentric, and forgetful of personal appearance in order to develop the properly disordered garret.

I am inclined to believe that much of what is called the asymmetrical viewpoint can be explained by what has been said concerning the sensitivity that forms the basis of sensual creativity. Possibly the artist's apparently odd way of looking at things derives more from the inherited and developed sensitivity which makes him more readily attuned to the subtleties of various sensations and impressions, than from an asymmetrical viewpoint different from the ordinary man in the street. In other words, the so-called asymmetrical mind or the peculiar way the creative person may look at things derives from a physically based sensitivity toward sensations of a certain type.

Regarding the role of disorder and chaos in the process of creativity one must be more careful. There are, first of all, different conceptions of the "orderly" and the "disorderly." What may be considered neat and orderly by one, may be considered the opposite by another who is a perfectionist. How essential, then, is disorder or chaos for creativity? And where does this disorder or chaos lie? Is it in the mind of the creative artist? Or is it outside him?

First of all, I do not think that a disorderly mind is necessarily a creative one. Such a mind may appear to be highly asymmetrical in the way it has of looking at things; and there may even be present the seeds of genius. Nevertheless, from a disordered mind, no matter how filled to overflowing it may be with a plethora of related and unrelated ideas, facts, and data, very little creative work actually seems to come forth. And creativity is a producing, a bringing forth, as well as a having. It is not sufficient to spawn new ideas with a reckless abandon, to write all sorts of novels in one's head. Creativity also means that those ideas must somehow be made creative, that is, something must come out of it all. Certainly one is familiar with persons who conceive vast and ambitious projects, but who are unable to bring any of them to maturity or completion. They may exhibit true genius, and yet exactly because of the "disordered" character of their minds, they find it impossible to create an order from their chaos. One of the reasons why such is often the case is, I think, because the disorder is not outside them but within them. They cannot order the facts, data, and material into an order, for they have not first put the house of their own mind in order.

There are also those who attempt to order too much. Thus they read and reread; they collect more and more related and unrelated data, often gaining richer and richer insight, until the task of ordering becomes absolutely Herculean. Such people are often perfectionists who go over the same material time after time, sifting each and every piece of real or imagined evidence with such meticulous care that they find it impossible to complete anything. They would seem to follow Rule VIII of Descartes' *Rules for the Direction of the Mind* almost to the letter; they enumerate and enumerate and enumerate every element which might possibly have a bearing upon the problem raised. The Germans sometimes call such a person *der ewiger Student,* the eternal student: he has not yet read absolutely everything he feels he should read for his dissertation or for his final examination.

Such people, indeed, produce a veritable chaos. And where there might not be enough chaos, they introduce even more disorder by the enumeration and repetition not only of those elements having a bearing upon the problem at hand, but also those that possibly might have a bearing. They give in all too readily to the fallacy of complete enumeration, and enumeration which can never be complete, particularly if it must include not only all that can, but also all that possibly might have a bearing on the problem under consideration.

The creative person manages to escape the rut of tedious, unproductive enumeration and repetition—the sort that can often succeed in creating a chaos where there is none or can unnecessarily complicate a relatively simple problem. In fact, it is even possible to create a pseudo problem in this way. One can, through the introduction of an impossible plethora of related and unrelated ideas, introduce a problem which is largely self-created. This is one of the reasons for the development of method. Creativity, as Poincaré correctly saw, necessarily implies choice. It is impossible to deal with absolutely everything. Enumeration can never be absolutely complete. There are elements which are and must be considered more or less important. There are limits to a man's powers of ordering, no matter how high may be his intelligence, no matter how great may be his assimilative powers. And the wholesale acceptance and introduction of a great many extraneous elements can easily create the chaos of a pseudo problem, namely, a problem which does not bear an answer by a finite mind.

This is the reason and the justification for method. A method represents a systematic but handy means of dealing with a chaos of facts and data. In artistic creativity it represents a style or a technique, the craft of the art. However, although the work of a particular artist is readily recognizable by its style or technique, this does not necessarily imply that the artist has a single and overbearing method which he applies indiscriminately to all the artistic problems he faces. He modifies his method to fit the problem, rather than the problem to fit the method.

This is, of course, the danger found in the use of a single method, arbitrarily chosen and rigorously applied. Since a method represents a systematic but handy means of sifting the disorder of the chaos, that process of sifting can be pushed one stage behind the perceptive process, so that it becomes a systematic means of presifting and presetting the data. A method cannot only accept and reject what has already been received; it can, through persistent use and practice, be pushed back to the level of receptivity as well, so that a person may fail to perceive what he does not wish to perceive, in accordance with his prechosen method. It is in this way, as we have seen, that a method, useful as it may be in dealing with a chaos, can degenerate into a bias or a prejudice that actually "desensitizes." The road from method to Procrusteanism can be traveled most quickly.

The real harm is caused when the process of dealing with the chaos, the means used for ordering that chaos in terms of the essential and the nonessential, is pushed back one stage, so that the method ceases to digest data, but rather "predigests" it. In this "preperceiving" the very physical basis for creativity can be undermined and subverted. For when this occurs the sensitivity of the artist to the subtleties of sensation or of the scientist to the relevant character of certain observations can be dulled. And when this desensitization occurs, the use of a method with reference to a chaos can end by stultifying, rather than by aiding, creativity. Method is able to assist in the ordering of a chaos; however, when it preorders that chaos, bias and a desensitizing of sensitivity can result.

There is another aspect of our image of the creative person, also touched upon earlier, which is related to the problem of order and disorder, and that is our image of the creative person as unkempt and nonconformist. The reasoning may be as follows: the artist is a creative person, and since the artist is often unkempt and nonconformist, then the creative person must be unkempt and nonconformist as well. It can, indeed, be that the creative person is forgetful of his personal appearance; however, this may arise from a quite different source than some endemic nonconformity. It may be true that the creative person appears different from other people; but this does not mean that he is a "professional" nonconformist. Thus no matter how high or how secluded his ivory tower may be, the creative person exists in society, and it is well and good for his creative life that he does. In any case, he does not spend his time doing exactly the opposite of what everybody else does. He does not display that type of nonconformity which sets out to do the opposite of what everyone else does. This is simply a new brand of conformism. One's activity is rigidly conformist when he must always be nonconformist.

Such is not the case with the creative person. It is true that he may appear nonconformist. However, this apparent nonconformity arises from a radically different source. His mind is occupied with something else. In other words, the creative person's deep and dedicated absorption in his work may best explain any failure on his part in the personal and social graces. Thus if he appears odd and eccentric to the majority of men, it may be because the majority of men are not so absolutely committed to their work or so passionately involved in what they are doing as is the creative person.

Certainly, the picture of the creative person as an eccentric nonconformist is overdrawn. On this score the exceptional cases tend to establish the rule. Indeed, a capacity to conform would seem to be part and parcel of any creative work, just as it is of life itself. For example, there is a certain necessary conformity involved in the self-imposed submission of brilliant new ideas to the cold, calculating eye of technique and self-criticism. Similarly, the creative person may exhibit a radical and avant-garde creativeness in his chosen field, and yet manifest a stubborn conservatism when it comes to certain political or social questions.

The image of the creative mind as eccentric or even somewhat disordered is part of the myth that surrounds the artist in our conception. It should be recognized, however, that it is largely a myth. Certainly it is not a necessary characteristic of the creative person that he be psychologically "abnormal." In fact, the creative person is very far from being mentally disordered or abnormal, as we have attempted to show above. Genius is not to madness near allied. There are at least two obvious differences between the "abnormality" of the creative person and that of the psychotic. First and most obvious is that the creative person is creative, whereas the psychotic is not. Secondly, the creative person seldom exhibits the patterned and tediously uncreative fixations of the psychotic. His thinking does not get into a tedious and unproductive rut. In this sense, of course, he is rigidly nonconformist. His thought may be patterned—through the development of his particular style or method or technique, or through the application of certain self-imposed rules—still these patterns do not determine his thinking. Rather, his thinking determines the patterns.

This patterning of thought and action is certainly a necessary part of life. Man is, as is often observed, a creature of habit. Indeed, habits are a man's salvation. If it were necessary to go consciously through all the particular operations involved in driving a car, a man would surely go mad. It would be sheer torture for him to think through or recall each and every little step involved in operating an automobile each and every time he took his seat behind the wheel—hence habits are a man's salvation. However, they can also be his damnation: when one multiplies the thousand and one operations which have thus become automatic through man's continuing response in terms of the same projections of goals and goods, we can appreciate how, in a civilization made more and more complex by the machines upon which man comes more and more to depend, the use which he makes of his intelligence can attain the rigid and mechanical character of just another machine.

The difficulty is not that man develops habits. This he must do, or he would surely go insane. And certainly men of other ages have developed habits of operation to function in an automatic fashion. Nevertheless, in a civilization where these habits can become as mechanical as the very machines upon which man comes to rely so heavily, even the use he makes of his intelligence can come to assume the rigid and mechanical reaction patterns common to his machines. Thus even his intelligent projections in terms of future goals and projects can become less humanly habitual and more and more mechanical in their character and performance.

This is an aspect of the "crisis of creativity" that cannot be safely ignored by modern psychology in its consideration of the nature and treatment of mental disorders in our age. However, it is less the crisis of the machine age than, as we have suggested, a crisis of life itself. For in a situation where a person's patterns of thought and reaction become more and more rigid and mechanistic both in their structure and function, it should not be surprising how modern man can slip off into the tediously uncreative fixations of neurosis and psychosis. However, this is not simply a question of creativity; it is also a question of life, of adaptation. The living organism is adaptive; it is not by necessity creatively so. By its very nature the living organism adapts, or, at least, attempts to adapt to different circumstances and situations. Generally it does this on a moment to moment basis. However, through the projective powers of his mind the human person is able to extend those projections into the future. These projections, based as they are upon past experience, knowledge, and thought, can develop into a specific and habitual pattern. They can be adaptive and creative. When they are *simply* adaptive, a certain "sameness" can creep into these adaptive responses. In this way patterns of thought and action can gain a rigidity and take on a primarily mechanical character which is removed only by degree from the fixed patterns of response to be encountered in the neurotic and the psychotic. In such cases life tends to fall into a rut, and thus into the all too depressive malaise of rigid reaction patterns to which is added the tedium of monotony through constant repetition. In this way a man, along with all the creative impulses in his life, becomes suffocated.

At first sight it may appear as though such a person has adapted well. However, although life is essentially adaptive it is not necessarily creative; and there are times when it must be creative. Habitual modes of thought and action will not even be "adaptive" in all situations. There are times when an organism can "overadapt," that is, it can proliferate structures and functions to such an extent that it may be easily subject to attack because of its highly overdeveloped complexity. One of the characteristics of life is its organic assimilative ability, whereby it takes into itself the surrounding disparate elements which it is able to use. In this way the organism grows and prospers. This is creative in such way that the unnecessary elaborations of structure and functions—particularly when they become purely mechanical—are not.

As we have urged above, creativity is life within a life, and in man this creative life must also be operative. It is not possible for a man simply to adapt in terms of the habitual functions and reaction patterns that he may develop in his process of adapting to his environment, particularly when this involves unnecessary proliferation or reactions purely mechanical in function. Many modern psychoses and neuroses issue exactly from this source. The crisis of creativity is not simply the crisis of the machine; it is also one of detaching the human mind from the mechanistic patterns of thinking that are common to the machine he uses. For such patterns of thinking lead to tedious and unproductive fixations. Certainly they cannot lead to creativity, or even to that creative adaptation which is at times necessary even for life itself.

But since creativity is a life within a life, it also represents the ordering of a chaos. Because this life is very often unconscious in its operation, this means that the ordering which takes place here is not the conscious ordering of a method. As we have seen, the unconscious represents a very special kind of "disorder"; it is a disorder which, through the selective forgetting and the unconscious association of ideas, creates an unconscious life as important for man's conscious life as the unconscious working of the heart or the digestive system is essential for the physical life of his body. Insofar, then, as life represents the ordering of a chaos, so also does creativity as a way of life represent such an ordering. This does not mean that the creative person must create the chaos, in the method of Descartes, for example, by tearing the problem into pieces. The chaos will take care of itself. When the creative person has involved himself deeply in any particular field of study or endeavor, a disorder will quickly present itself, one which will offer to him wide latitude in the creative use of both conscious and, equally important, unconscious mind.

CREATIVITY AND SUFFERING

Possibly there is no philosopher in modern times who expresses the sufferings of the creative person with as much personal intensity or with such poignancy as does the Danish philosopher, Sören Kierkegaard (1813-1855). For various reasons he is a very difficult figure to classify. One hardly knows whether to consider him a writer of great wit and charm, a perceptive and subtle dialectician, or a theologian of truly Christian proportions.

Kierkegaard would classify himself as, from first to last, primarily a religious author.[16] Yet he remains an author who, throughout his works and at every stage of his writings, constantly reiterates the theme of a sensitive and creative man suffering.

It is not our task here to determine the causes of the severe melancholy under which he labored, its physical or psychological basis;[17] the fact that it was reinforced by a belief that his family suffered under a curse—because his father had cursed God in his youth;[18] nor is it necessary to go into the reasons why Kierkegaard systematically refused to seek solace from his melancholic loneliness through art (the aesthetic) or through marriage (the ethical).

His life he had dedicated to one, single ideal, that is, to becoming a Christian. Nevertheless, this single-minded, dedicated pursuit of what it means to be a Christian did not seem to offer any relief, or did it seem to provide any release from the extreme depths of his melancholy.

And yet, Kierkegaard was able to find some relief from the deep and lonely suffering that troubled his spirit, in a way that was thoroughly in accord with his ideal. He found this relief in the very creativity whereby he attempted to unburden himself of his sufferings and to express the full personal significance of his one and only ideal. As he says,

Only when I am producing do I feel well. Then I forget all the discomforts of life, all suffering, then am I in my thought and happy. If I let it alone even for a couple of days I immediately get ill, overwhelmed, troubled, my head heavy and burdened.[19]

From this it should not be thought that Kierkegaard's creative productivity was pursued or effected *because of* his various personal woes and sufferings. Rather, one would have to say that he was able to function creatively *in spite of* his personal sufferings and melancholy. For as soon as he ceased his creative work, even for a moment, his melancholy took over again. In other words, it was not because of the sufferings, prompted at least in part by the dreary melancholy under which he labored, that he was able to produce such works of compelling genius. Rather, it was because of his ability to transcend the melancholy that he was able to create as he did. And in thus overcoming such powerful psychological and even physical disabilities through creative work, not only did they cease to trouble him with their accustomed force, but also were even replaced by a certain elation.

This is certainly not an isolated phenomenon, this relation between suffering and creativity; and it follows naturally from what has been said concerning sensual creativity and sensitivity. For example, this relation between suffering and creativity exists even at the level of such primarily physical pursuits as sports. For what is, after all, the difference between a mediocre athlete and a champion athlete? One of those differences is the ability of the champion to withstand pain. This is one of the reasons for the punishing self-discipline of training which the athlete undertakes with such systematic ardor. For the champion athlete is one who must push his body, his muscles, his whole frame, beyond the point of normal endurance.

He must be able to make that last extra effort, that last lunge toward the tape, when his lungs are breathing fire and his legs feel like lead weights. He must push himself, force himself beyond the breaking point, the point beyond which he is sure he cannot go. This involves pain. This is one of the reasons why the athlete trains, disciplines, toughens himself to his task, so that he will become inured to this pain. He will be aware of the pain, as he stretches himself to the limit of his endurance. And yet, the pain will be completely forgotten, not so much because of the pleasure of victory—for he may not be victorious—or simply in the pleasure which comes from overcoming the pain involved in pushing his body to the ultimate reaches of its endurance. For it is not the pain that is somehow pleasurable, or even simply the overcoming of the pain. The athlete is not a masochist. The element of pleasure is produced in the overcoming of this pain necessarily involved in overcoming the particular obstacle or difficulty in the sport.

Thus neither is the mountain climber simply a masochist. The pain he endures in his attempt to surmount the obstacle of the mountain before him is not enjoyed for its own sake. Nor does he endure this pain simply for the rewarding experience of standing on the top of the mountain, or for the view. The pleasure the mountaineer takes in climbing mountains is not simply the pleasure in having overcome the mountain, but rather in actually overcoming the obstacle of his own painful fear, in actually overcoming the pain involved in the ascent. It is this *overcoming* that produces the pleasure of climbing mountains.

This element of the painful, as well as that of personal dedication, cannot be dissociated from the creative process, whether that creativity be in athletic competition, in art, or in science. It is not a part of that process in the sense that it is required for creativity in a certain field or discipline, in the same way that passionate dedication is required. Rather, pain at the physical level in sports, or suffering at a psychic level, represents a backdrop against which, or an obstacle over which, creativity must triumph. Whether this element of the painful involves sitting in front of an easel for many hours every day or pushing the human body to the limits of its powers in athletic competition, pain is present and nevertheless overcome. And in this overcoming is contained much of the pleasure of sports and the elation of creative work.

Pleasure and pain are often thought of in terms of opposites. This pairing off of pleasure and pain in the determination of that which is good and bad in a moral sense can be traced from Epicurus and the later atomists to Democritus, the father of atomism, and on to David Hume. However, as becomes clear, pleasure and pain cannot be paired off that easily—one against the other—for both together make up the fabric of human existence. And there is at least one human activity wherein they are closely bound together, namely, that of creativity. And certainly if creativity is a way of life, or a life within a life, this intimate association of pleasure and pain in creativity should not surprise.

That pain is necessarily associated with life can be seen in the phenomenon of adaptation, one of the fundamental characteristics of life itself. For were it not for the factor of pain, the organism would have no way of knowing that its life was being threatened, whether externally by some enemy or internally through some organic malfunction. It is true that there are those with low thresholds of pain, and these and other facts would tend to indicate that pain is not an infallible guide to physical dangers, whether internal or external. Thus we might feel no pain in taking a toxic poison, and the pain might only be felt too late to save the organism.

But even though pain may not be an infallible guide for dangers to life, it nevertheless remains a part of that adaptive process associated with life. In fact, it might be argued that it is more closely associated with life than is pleasure. Indeed, the pleasure one may receive cannot easily be dissociated from pain in many cases. It is no accident that the early German romantics tended to associate love (pleasure) and death (pain). Freud also insisted upon the intimate connection between the pleasure instinct (the libido) and the death instinct.

There is a definite and close relationship between pain and life. Not that life is simply pain and suffering. For if it is correct to say that one of the necessary characteristics of life is adaptation, then one can readily understand how a certain pleasure, a certain sense of well-being can occur when that which has caused the pain has been overcome by successful adaptation. This feeling of well-being and exhilaration can also be physical, as, for example, when one recovers from a serious illness or an operation. This same feeling of elation and exhilaration is also associated with creativity, both during and immediately following the creative activity, despite the painful discomfort or frustrating obstacles which one may have to overcome.

There are, however, good and bad effects to pain, and to the overcoming of that pain through adaptation, whether that adaptation be creative or not. Thus, for example, pain on the physical level signifies the alarm which the organism registers in the face of a threat to its existence. Let us say that the threat is a particular disease. Now when health has been restored to the organism, the effects of that disease nonetheless remain. The organism is no longer the same

after, as it was before the onset of the disease. First of all,
it has been weakened from its struggle with the disease.
Secondly, the organism is often rendered immune to future
recurrences of the same disease. This latter represents the
principle behind immunization, namely, the introduction
of the disease in smaller doses into the organism in order
to prevent a serious case of that disease.

There is also another effect following upon this disease-
pain-recovery cycle, one more directly the result of the pain
itself, and that is *sympathy*. This means, for example, that
if we ourselves have suffered through a particular illness,
we are more apt to appreciate the sufferings which others
may be going through. This is why it is often said that the
doctor who has never been sick has less understanding and
less sympathy for the illnesses of his patients than one who
has been seriously ill.

In creativity and creative work pain can also have both
a good and a bad effect. In the first place, it must be recognized that pain is something which for the creative person
is inevitable. It is inevitable that his "threshold of suffering" will be lower because of, and in accordance with his
greater sensitivity. This is another way that pain and suffering accompany, and indeed must accompany, the creative
process. The greater sensitivity of the artist necessarily
exacts its price, and that price is a lower threshold for pain
and suffering.

There are those who would attempt to banish all pain
from the lives of man. This will never be completely possible, because of the nature of life and of adaptation, as
we have seen; nevertheless, more and more drugs appear
on the market providing modern medical science with the
means of reducing the areas of pain to a minimum. And
insofar as these drugs ameliorate or actually remove the

senseless, stupefying, the cruel pain of the last stages of certain diseases or certain extremely painful operations, on this score one could have no quarrel with the pharmaceutical industries. Yet, the war on pain can be carried too far. Pain is not the ultimate evil. It is a part, and a not unimportant part, of the adaptive process which is life itself. It is only the senseless, stupefying pain, cruelly inflicted and unresignedly borne, which poses the most serious problem for the philosopher and the theologian.

In a very real sense, to banish all pain would be to banish creativity. For if every possibility for pain or suffering were banished, the very sensitivity that is at the root of pain and suffering, but also is the physical basis for the creative process, would likewise be dulled. The suffering of which Kierkegaard speaks is a necessary consequence of the sensitivity of the creative person. The creative person does not attempt to banish pain. He does not seek a resort from pain in the safety and security of stupefying drugs. And even those artists who have made use of drugs or drink to gain or regain that level of physical elation at which they may work best do not do so in order to substitute one form of stupefaction for another. The creative person does not seek to banish pain. He seeks to overcome the suffering, and this through creativity, a creativity which requires the heightened sensitivity, and which is the very cause of that pain and suffering in the first place.

It is necessary, however, to make a distinction between pain and suffering. In a real sense only a man can suffer. An animal may feel pain, but it cannot suffer. It cannot suffer exactly because it is unable to realize the significance of what is happening to it. The dog does not know that the weight of a child standing on its paw will not cripple it for life. It feels the pain and reacts with a yelp. The dog's reaction is, as we say, instinctive. It cannot, like a man on a crowded bus, whose foot is being crushed by a large woman holding a bag of groceries, smile benignly and say that it is nothing. The man can patiently suffer the pain, realizing that although his corns will never again be the same, he will live through the experience. The dog cannot be so sure. It may feel the pain, but because it fails to realize the significance of what is really happening, it cannot suffer. The man is able to overcome the pain with a smile. And one might say that there is something almost creative about that smile. Only a man of great politeness, only a gentleman, could smile in such trying circumstances.

There are, as we have observed, both good and bad effects in the overcoming of the pain associated with physical illness. In the same way there are good and bad effects flowing from the overcoming of the suffering or discomfort associated with creative work. Indeed, the overcoming can, like the physical process of immunization, produce the "second nature" of a truly free-flowing style; however, it can also degenerate into the rut of a system or a method. In other words, it is possible for productivity to become automatic, so much "second nature" that it can become wholly mechanical. The creative person can develop a style, one that is less a style and more a system or method, which systematically and even aprioristically structures and impedes the flow of original ideas. And because of the difficulty—and even the anguish which may accompany the changing of one's approach, one's presuppositions, or basic way of looking at problems—one's activity can easily become stereotyped; fixed ideas, ingrained; a style, a strait jacket. The artist must develop a style; and yet, to remain genuinely creative that style may never degenerate into a rigid system for pre-set categories. As we have observed, the thinking of the creative person must determine the patterns, not the patterns his thinking.

The element of the painful enters into the appreciation as well as into the production of the arts. For example, the element of the painful functions in music as dissonance; in painting, as the ugly; in sculpture, as the grotesque. The dissonant or the ugly are in a certain way "painful," and yet they are part and parcel of the work of art as a whole. In fact, they make up our total enjoyment of the work of art. Dissonance, one might say, represents the spice of variety in music. If all music were composed of sweet and melodious harmonies, we should soon become bored with its saccharine sweetness. The dissonances capture our attention, and we take pleasure in their resolution. It is in this way that they form a part and contribute to the beauty of the whole composition.

Taking a cue from music, however, we note that what is considered consonant and dissonant can change with time and with education. Sensitivity, though probably hereditary in basis, can be educated. Thus for fourteenth-century ears, the major third, which we consider consonant, was then considered a dissonance; and the so-called open fifth was considered consonant. Today we should tend to consider the relative consonance and dissonance of the two intervals as exactly the opposite.

There is another way whereby the element of the painful or suffering may enter the life of the creative person. During and immediately after the creative production of something, there will often occur a feeling of elation and pleasure at having overcome a particular obstacle or difficulty, whether artistic, intellectual, or scientific. Nevertheless, this feeling is generally short-lived. For very soon the creative person becomes his own critic. He stands back and takes a critical look at his creation. If he is truly honest with himself, he is his best critic. For immediately he sees that his work is not as perfect as it might have been. He did not succeed in expressing the whole of his creative idea with the completeness and richness that he might have desired. He may even feel that he has failed completely. During and immediately after his creative activity, he was blinded to the defects of his work by the elation and the sense of satisfaction that accompanied and immediately followed the overcoming of the obstacles he faced. However, his elation often quickly turns to dejection; his feeling of self-satisfaction, to depression.

Curiously, the suffering associated with such feelings of failure is as necessary as it is valuable to the life of the creative person. For it is this sense of failure and frustration which drives him ever forward in his attempt to reach the perfection of expression that he desires. Possibly he will succeed next time. Indeed, were the creative person perfectly and permanently satisfied with his creation, he might cease this endless striving; he might rest satisfied with his one achievement. He might slip into an easy complacency that would spell the end of his creative life within a life, which is fostered as much by failures and bad starts as by successes and triumphs.

This feeling of frustration and failure can be compounded by the fact that even what he may have brought forth with such personal difficulty and hardship to himself goes unappreciated by the majority of his contemporaries. It may not represent the perfect expression or complete embodiment of his idea; yet he still knows the effort that the work, imperfect though it is, has cost him.

But this simply constitutes a necessary part of his creative life, and he would not wish it any different. He may seek, in various ways, solace for what he considers his personal failure or the apathy of an unappreciative audience in the artificially induced well-being of drugs or drink, in professional and personal friendships, and so forth. However, it will be to no avail, at least so far as his creative life is concerned. For the elements of pain and suffering belong of necessity to that life which is a life within a life. The pain and suffering he feels arise from both the sensitivity that is his, and from the genuine love and passionate dedication he brings to that area of study or work wherein he labors. This passionate dedication itself necessarily involves suffering; it involves the pain of a great deal of hard labor and self-discipline, the frustration of preliminary failures, and the like. It is, of course, true that the creative person is able to overcome some of the more painful aspects associated with his creative life because of his strong personal dedication. And he is able to work in spite of the personally painful elements associated with self-discipline and the failures he meets; and it is in this "overcoming" that the peculiar elation of creativity consists. Suffering and disappointment cannot be banished from his life. No matter how externally successful he may become, the feelings of elation from accomplishment pass, and there remains the gnawing sense of failure.

It may be that depth psychology can offer something of a clue to the sensitivity which is the strength and yet the weakness of the creative person. The insensitive person, it might be said, is one who has successfully hidden his ego behind several layers of protective psychic skin; whereas the sensitive person is one who "wears his ego on his sleeve." This situation has the advantage of permitting the sensitive person to feel things more personally and more strongly; however, it also has the disadvantage of making him feel those things more painfully.

Whether this is the ultimate explanation for sensitivity in the creative person is difficult to determine. For, after all, the threshold of pain and hence that of sensitivity can be raised or lowered through training and education, even through sickness and disease. But it seems doubtful that the sensitivity of the scientist, namely, the sensitivity necessary to appreciate the relevant scientific character of a particular experiment or observation, which is largely the result of education, is somehow determined by the stratum at which the ego places itself in the personality. It is certainly true that the scientist must be able to realize when he "has" something. Nevertheless, it seems to me doubtful that this necessarily implies the "ego exposure" described above. The sensitivity of the scientist to discoveries in his science rests largely upon education and experience. And even in the creative artist, if we are correct in our analysis of sensual creativity, it would seem that such sensitivity, physically based in origin and nature, is largely hereditary. It may, indeed, be that the sensitive artist "wears his ego on his sleeve"; however, the reason for this may also find its basis in a physically grounded sensitivity.

Suffering, then, remains the ineluctable fate from which the creative person does not, indeed cannot, escape. The sensitivity that gives rise to it, whatever may be its ultimate source or basis, is both the strength of the creative person and his weakness. To banish this weakness may be to banish his strength. The creative person, like a Samson, is always in danger of losing his strength in losing his weakness.

6
Conclusion

In the preceding pages I have attempted to analyze the nature and the historical roots of the phenomenon which has been termed the crisis of creativity. It is a crisis of man's thinking and decision-making ability and as such represents the crisis of man himself, since these powers of thinking things through, and then deciding the matter of his own destiny upon the basis of such thinking, represent the highest powers possessed by man.

Nevertheless, if man is to think things through and then decide the matter of his own destiny in a creative manner —namely, if man is to overcome this crisis that is, has been, and always will be his in every age—then it is also necessary for him to understand something of the nature and operation of creativity itself. Hence, besides tracing this crisis back to its roots in Western thought, I have also attempted to analyze the elements involved in the creative process, and to determine something of their mode of operation.

One of the most important elements, as we have seen, is the unconscious, a "faculty" which proves impervious to direct analysis. From the point of view of consciousness this "faculty" of the unconscious may appear to be nothing at all. For when conscious thought attempts to look

167

into the unconscious and its operations it sees literally *nothing*. This is one reason why creativity, when it actually occurs, may appear to come from "nothing." The conscious mind is generally unaware of the largely unconscious preparation of the materials involved in the creative process. From the point of view of consciousness, then, creativity appears to arise *ex nihilo*. There was nothing like it existing before, nothing like it produced before. It is a new creation. Indeed, it does not arise, as it may appear to arise, *absolutely* from nothing or from nowhere; as if there were no pre-existent materials from which the particular creative production was drawn or fashioned, such as colors, sounds, language, marble, ideas, or whatever. Still, from the point of view of consciousness, it may appear to arise *ex nihilo*.

For this reason it is not surprising that many artists and creative persons in different fields have come to look upon their creative gifts as something quasi divine in origin. Human creativity is, after all, like divine creativity—creative. Indeed, the theologian tends to describe God's "creativity" as a *creatio ex nihilo*, which, as we have seen, is exactly the way an artist's creativity may appear to consciousness, as coming from "nothing" (*ex nihilo*).

And certainly from the way creativity, whether artistic or scientific, is able to transform the life, the vision, and the world of mankind, it is understandable that the particular creative person may come to look upon his creative gift as something somehow divinely given, a sort of mysterious or even mystical power whose source and nature are not to be questioned. And this possibility of divine inspiration is simply not to be ruled out, as, for example, religious or biblical inspiration, in the technical sense of that word. Though even here the power of creativity in man remains something peculiarly human, the human author of the sacred book remains an author in the fully, and humanly, creative sense.

Indeed, human creativity may have about it something of the divine, and may also appear to consciousness as certainly arising from "nowhere." However, the similarity between human and divine creativity may also lead to the conclusion that man's ability to create is the greatest and highest power he possesses, and that it is in the development of this power that the fulfillment of his greatest potentialities, both socially and personally, actually lies.

Creativity ministers to the benefit of society through the solution of a wide variety of problems, scientific, technological, sociological, and so forth; it ministers to the good of society through the production of works of art and beauty which are able to carry man beyond the present and immediate needs of his life and to fill that life with objects of interest and beauty. But creativity also ministers to the good of the individual creative person as well, by filling that gap, that "nothing," within his own being. The sense of elation which accompanies creative work results in great measure from the successful filling of this gap, by fulfilling a basic need in the creative individual's own life. This sense of elation and the heightened consciousness involved in actual creative work are both the cause and the effect of creativity: the cause of creativity inasmuch as by developing to the full his creative potentialities, it represents the result of that passionate dedication whereby the creative person seeks to fill that gap within himself; the effect of creativity in that this feeling of elation results, in its turn, from the successful overcoming of a particular obstacle or problem.

It is this passionate interest of dedication in something considered eminently worthwhile that is at the heart of all creative work and that produces the high emotional level, the heightened consciousness, in which the rich association of ideas, so necessary to the creative process, tends to occur. It is this, too, that drives a man ever onward in search of a more adequate expression of his creative ideas, to seek creative solutions to the problems that face him, as well as mankind, in every age and in every area of work and study.

Creativity is the inner life of man himself, a life within a life. This life manifests itself in a type of "adaptation" which goes beyond the more immediate and day-to-day concerns of man to a new, original, and stimulating fulfillment of his future.

Notes

NOTES TO CHAPTER 2

1. Aristotle, *Metaphysics* D, 3; 1005b, 2-7. See also *Meta.* A, 3; 995a, 12-14.
2. *Meta.* A, 1; 993b, 20-21. Much less could it be a "productive science," which is "the reasoned state of capacity to make." *Eth. Nic.* VI, 4; 1140a, 4-5. Indeed, in the *Rhetoric* Aristotle refers to the "science of logic" (*Rhet.* I, 4; 1359b, 9-12); still he fails to explain what sort of science it is. It does apparently combine with the ethical branch of politics to form what is called rhetoric. Aristotle may here be thinking of the Sophists.
3. Aristotle, *An. Post.* I, 2; 71b, 17.
4. *Ibid.,* I, 1; 71a, 1.
5. *Ibid.,* I, 1; 72b, 40.
6. *Ibid.,* I, 13; 78a, 30 ff.
7. *Ibid.,* II, 16; 98b, 20.
8. *Aristotle, An. Pr.* I, 4; 25b, 35-39 (Ross, tr.). Jan Lukasiewicz, in *Aristotle's Syllogistic: From the Standpoint of Modern Formal Logic* (2 ed.; Oxford: Clarendon Press, 1957), pp. 21-23, insists that the original form of the Aristotelian syllogism was not "All B is A, All C is B, Ergo, all C is A," but rather something more closely corresponding to modern logic. And unlike the later Aristotelians Aristotle, more often than not, used letters rather than words.
9. *Ibid.,* I, 32; 47a, 40.
10. Aristotle, *An. Post.* I, 6; 75a, 36-37.
11. *Ibid.,* I, 6; 75a, 12-15.
12. γὰρ τὰ αἴτια τὰ μεσα ἰδών: Aristotle, *An. Post.* I, 34; 89b, 16. A common criticism of the Aristotelian syllogism is noted

by W. D. Ross, *Aristotle* (New York: Meridian, 1959), p. 41, where he says it is untrue to state that one must somehow know C (which is a B) in order to say that B is A in the syllogism "All B is A, All C is B, All C is A." All that is needed to produce a "genuine movement of thought" is the knowledge that C has the essential attributes of B. It is not necessary to know whether it has all the actual properties of B. Similarly, he notes, it is not necessary to examine all the instances of B to say that B is A, so long as we know basically what sets off B from everything else.

13. Aristotle, *An. Post.* I, 34, 89b, 10-15.
14. *Ibid.*, II, 3; 90a, 35.
15. *Ibid.*, I, 18, 81a, 38-81b, 6.
16. *Ibid.*, I, 10; 76a, 31.
17. *Ibid.*, I, 12; 77b, 1.
18. Descartes, *Regulae ad Directionem Ingenii,* ed. H. Gouhier (3 ed.; Paris: Vrin, 1959), p. 34. The text is that of the standard Adam and Tannery edition, *Oeuvres de Descartes* (Paris: Cerf, 1908), pp. 359-469.
19. *Ibid.*, p. 35.
20. *Ibid.*, p. 46.
21. *Ibid.*, p. 80.
22. *Ibid.*, p. 39. He notes that we experience what we perceive with the senses, and the intellect contemplating itself reflexively. *Ibid.*, p. 100.
23. *Ibid.*, p. 39.
24. *Ibid.*, p. 44.
25. René Descartes, *Discours de la Méthode,* text and commentary by E. Gilson (Paris: Vrin, 1947), pp. 18-19.
26. *Ibid.*, p. 37. Descartes makes only one exception to this rule, and that is in the use of *hypothesis.* One may make use of probable conjectures (*conjecturae)* so long as credence is not given to them. *Regulae,* p. 101.
27. The importance of beginning with the simple is treated in Rules V and X; see especially p. 80 of the *Regulae.* In Rule VI Descartes suggests that the secret of the method (almost everything is the "secret of the method") is marking out what is most absolute. *Ibid.*, p. 57.

28. Descartes, *Discours,* pp. 18-19.
29. Descartes, *Regulae,* p. 81.
30. *Ibid.,* p. 130.
31. *Ibid.,* p. 51.
32. *Ibid.,* pp. 82-83. Descartes makes the same point in the *Discours (op. cit.,* p. 17), as does the author in his preface to the *Principles of Philosophy,* where he speaks of logic (dialectics) as means of making things understood by others, nothing more. Descartes refers to this as the "corruption of good sense *(bon sens).*"
33. Descartes, *Discours,* p. 49.
34. Descartes, *Regulae,* p. 94.
35. *Ibid.,* p. 73.
36. *Ibid.,* p. 120.
37. Francis Bacon, *Works,* eds. Spedding, Ellis, and Heath (London:Longman, 1858), I, 158 (Book I, Aphorism 14).
38. *Ibid.,* I, 159 (Bk. I, Aph. 19).
39. *Ibid.,* I, 168-169 (Bk. I, 51).
40. *Ibid.,* I, 494 (Bk. II, ch. 1).
41. *Ibid.,* I, 540-541 (Bk. III, ch. 1).
42. *Ibid.,* I, 547 (Bk. III, ch. 3).
43. See Bk. III, ch. 5 and 6. (Bacon, *Works,* I, 571 ff.).
44. Bacon, *Works,* I, 549-550.
45. *Ibid.,* I, 567.
46. *Ibid.,* I, 494.
47. *Ibid.,* I, 518.

NOTES TO CHAPTER 3

1. Francis Bacon, *Works,* eds. Spedding, Ellis, and Heath (London: Longman, 1858), I, 576 ff.
2. Norbert Wiener, *The Human Use of Human Beings* (2 ed.; Garden City: Doubleday Anchor Books, 1954), p. 33.
3. See J. W. Getzels and P. W. Jackson, *Creativity and Intelligence* (New York: Wiley, 1962).
4. Friedrich von Schlegel, *Kritische Schriften,* ed. W. Rasch (München: Hanser, 1938), p. 21.

Notes to Chapter 4

1. Immanuel Kant, *Werke in sechs Bänden,* ed. W. Weischedel (Darmstadt: Wissenschaftliche Buchgesellschaft, 1957), VI, 544-545.
2. ". . . das belebende Prinzip im Gemüte." Kant, *Werke,* V, 413.
3. Kant, *Werke,* VI, 544.
4. Immanuel Kant, *Kritik der reinen Vernunft,* ed. R. Schmidt (2 ed.; Hamburg: Meiner, 1956), A 78, B 102; henceforth cited *K.d.r.V.*
5. Kant, *K.d.r.V.,* B 152.
6. Kant, *Werke,* V, 414; see particularly Number 49 of the *Kritik der Urteilskraft;* and compare this with the summary treatment in the Anthropologie, Number 25 (*Werke,* VI, 466).
7. *Ibid.,* V, 417-418.
8. *Ibid.,* V, 414.
9. *Ibid.,* V, 420. One can almost hear the distinction between "emotive" and "scientific" language being enunciated here by Kant, long before the "New Criticism."
10. Kant, *K.d.r.V.,* B 152.
11. *Ibid.,* A 201, B 246.
12. Kant, *Werke,* VI, 546.
13. Kant, *K.d.r.V.,* B 164.
14. *Ibid.,* A 120 n. Or as Kant expressed it in the second edition of the "Transcendental Deduction of the Categories," without this synthesis of apprehension, there is no *definite* intuition: ". . . aber ohne Verbindung des Mannigfaltigen in derselben, mithin noch gar keine *bestimmte* Anschauung enthält . . ." (*K.d.r.V.,* B 154). The italics are, significantly, Kant's own.
15. *Ibid.,* A 145, B 185.
16. Kant, *Werke,* V, 418.
17. Kant, *K.d.r.V.,* A ix.
18. I do not think that this differs essentially from the view taken by Kant in his "anticipations of Perception" (*K.d.r.V.,*

A 166, B 206 ff), namely, that there is a certain degree of intensive magnitude to any and every sensation, except Kant seems to presuppose that the degree of a sensation could be "zero."

19. See, for example, his "One of the Difficulties of Psychoanalysis" (1917), collected in Sigmund Freud, *On Creativity and the Unconscious* (New York: Harper and Row, 1958), p. 9. Although in a work entitled "The Unconscious" (1915) Freud, quoting Kant, observes that mental processes are themselves unconscious. See *Great Books* (Chicago: Encyclopedia Britannica, 1952), vol. LIV: Freud, p. 430.

20. Leibnitz, *Monadology,* Number 14. G. W. Leibnitz, *Principes de la Nature et de la Grace, Principes de la Philosophie ou Monadologie,* ed. Λ. Robinet (Paris: Presses Universitaires de France, 1954), p. 77.

21. Leibnitz, *Monadology,* Number 21 (*ibid.,* pp. 81-82).

22. Freud, *On Creativity and the Unconscious,* p. 217.

23. *Ibid.,* p. 186.

24. Dryden, *Absalom and Achitophel,* I, 163-164.

25. *Great Books,* LIV, 431 ff.

26. See the excellent article by Rollo May, "The Nature of Creativity," *Creativity and its Cultivation* (New York: Harper, 1959), pp. 55-68.

27. *Great Books,* LIV, 428.

28. Locke, *Essay,* II, x, 1. John Locke, *An Essay Concerning Human Understanding,* ed. A. C. Fraser (New York: Dover, 1959), I, 193.

29. *Ibid.,* II, x, 5 (I, 196).

30. William James, *The Principles of Psychology* (New York: Dover, 1950), I, 643.

31. Locke, *Essay,* II, x, 6 (I, 680).

32. James, *Principles of Psychology,* I, 680.

33. *Ibid.,* I, 684.

34. This would seem to be one of the necessary requirements for developing a species of "computer consciousness" in the machines. See, for example, the fascinating work by J. T. Culbertson, *The Minds of Robots* (Urbana: University of Illinois Press, 1963). The author carefully notes that the sort of "consciousness" which he would attempt to

simulate mechanically would not be constructed on anatomical or physiological models of the human brain. Any resemblance between the human brain and the "brain" of the computer, he explains, would be "incidental." *Ibid.*, pp. 248-249.

35. Plato, *Phaedo*, 73-76.
36. Aristotle, *De Memoria* II, 451b, 18-20.
37. Locke, *Essay*, II, xxxiii, 5 (I, 529).
38. *Ibid.*, II, xxxiii, 8 (I, 531).
39. David Hume, *A Treatise of Human Nature*, ed. L. A. Selby-Bigge (Oxford: Clarendon Press, 1888), I, 1, 3, p. 9.
40. *Ibid.*, I, 1, 4 (pp. 10-13).
41. *Ibid.*, II, 1, 4 (p. 283).
42. *Ibid.*, II, 1, 5 (p. 286).
43. *Ibid.*, II, 1, 5 (p. 289).
44. *Ibid.*, II, 1, 6 (p. 283).
45. David Hume, *Enquiry concerning Human Understanding*, VII, 1; in D. C. Yalden-Thomson, *Hume: Theory of Knowledge* (Edinburgh: Nelson, 1951), p. 64.
46. The attack on universals was typical of seventeenth-century philosophy. Identifying the origin and nature of "transcendentals" with "abstract universals" is highly problematic in metaphysics.
47. Spinoza, *Ethics*, II, 50, schol. 1. J. van Vloten and J. P. N. Land (eds.), *Benedicti de Spinoza Opera*, 2 vols. (3 ed.; Hague: Nijhoff, 1914), I, 105.
48. *Ibid.*, II, 17, schol.
49. *Ibid.*, II, 18, schol.
50. *Ibid.*, II, 50, schol. 1.
51. D. A. Schon, *Displacement of Concepts* (London: Tavislock, 1963).

NOTES TO CHAPTER 5

1. See H. Poincaré, *The Foundations of Science* (Lancaster, Pa.: Science Press, 1946), pp. 383-394.
2. *Ibid.*, p. 387.
3. *Ibid.*, p. 388.

4. *Ibid.*
5. *Ibid.*, p. 390.
6. *Ibid.*, p. 386.
7. D. A. Schon, *Displacement of Concepts* (London: Tavis-lock, 1963). Such an approach toward understanding creativity seems to apply best to problems of mechanical inventiveness.
8. See W. J. J. Gordon, *Synectics: The Development of Creative Capacity* (New York: Harper, 1961), pp. 18, 28, though similar uses of personification and analogy for the purposes of discovery can be found throughout the book.
9. Henri Bergson, *L'Évolution Créatrice* (86 ed.; Paris: Presses Universitaires de France, 1959), pp. 247-248 n.
10. *Ibid.*, p. 261.
11. *Ibid.*, p. 263.
12. *Ibid.*, p. 266.
13. Still, Bergson denies "finality" to the evolutionary process, at least in any technical sense of that word. Life, he feels, transcends finality. *Ibid.*, p. 266. Nevertheless, here one cannot help being reminded very strongly of Hegel's Absolute Spirit, which is at the end of a long process of development and yet is and must be present at each and every stage of the process in order to make that process possible. This is the basic argument of his *Phenomenology of Spirit*. One can see this same idea mirrored in the writings of Pierre Teilhard de Chardin, particularly in his *Phenomenon of Man*.
14. ". . . l'intuition est l'esprit même et, en un certain sense, le vie même. . . ." *Ibid.*, p. 268.
15. "On ne le reconnaît qu'en se plaçant dans l'intuition pour aller de là à l'intelligence, car de l'intelligence on ne passera jamais à l'intuition." *Ibid.*, p. 268.
16. "I became an author, but I turned aside to become a religious author." *The Journals of Sören Kierkegaard*, ed. A. Dru (London: Oxford University Press, 1938), Number 1180 (p. 426); see also 795 (p. 253) and 1294 (p. 491).
17. *Ibid.*, Number 600 (pp. 169-170).
18. *Ibid.*, Number 243 (p. 66); 556 (p. 150).
19. *Ibid.*, Number 627 (p. 191). Similarly, "A poet is often a

sufferer in existence, but what we reflect upon is the poetic productivity which is thereby brought about. The existing poet who suffers in his existence does not really comprehend his suffering, he does not penetrate more and more deeply into it, but in his suffering he seeks a way from the suffering and finds ease in poetic production, in the poetic anticipation of a more perfect, i.e., a happier, order of things." Kierkegaard, *Concluding Unscientific Postscript*, D. F. Swenson (tr.) (Princeton: University Press, 1941), p. 397 and ff.

Bibliography

Bacon, Francis. *Works*, eds. Spedding, Ellis, and Heath. 14 vols. London: Longmans, 1858.

Bergson, Henri. *L'Évolution Créatrice*. 86 ed. Paris: Presses Universitaires de France, 1959.

Culbertson, J. T. *The Minds of Robots*. Urbana: University of Illinois Press, 1963.

Descartes, René. *Discours de la Methode*, text and commentary by E. Gilson. Paris: Vrin, 1947.

————. *Regulae ad Directionem Ingenii*, ed. H. Gouhier. 3 ed. Paris: Vrin, 1959.

Freud, Sigmund. *On Creativity and the Unconscious*, ed. Benjamin Nelson. New York: Harper Torchbooks, 1958.

————. "The Unconscious," *Great Books*. Chicago: Encyclopedia Britannica, 1952; vol. LIV: Freud, pp. 428-443.

Getzels, J. W. and Jackson, P. W. *Creativity and Intelligence*. New York: Wiley, 1962.

Gordon, W. J. J. *Synectics: The Development of Creative Capacity*. New York: Harper, 1961.

Hume, David. "Enquiry Concerning Human Understanding," in D. C. Yalden-Thomson. *Hume: Theory of Knowledge*. Edinburgh: Nelson, 1951, pp. 1-176.

————. *A Treatise of Human Nature*, ed. L. A. Selby-Bigge. Oxford: Clarendon Press, 1888.

James, William. *The Principles of Psychology*. 2 vols. New York: Dover, 1950.

Kant, Immanuel. *Kritik der reinen Vernunft*, ed. R. Schmidt. 2 ed. Hamburg: Meiner, 1956.

————. "Anthropologie in pragmatischer Hinsicht," *Werke in sechs Bänden*, ed. W. Weischedel. Darmstadt: Wissenschaftliche Buchgesellschaft, 1957, VI, 395-690.

179

Kierkegaard, Sören. *Concluding Unscientific Postcript*. Princeton, N.J.: Princeton University Press, 1941.

——. *The Journals*, ed. A. Dru. London: Oxford University Press, 1938.

Leibnitz, G. W. *Principes de la Nature et de la Grace, Principes de la Philosophie ou Monadologie*, ed. A. Robinet. Paris: Presses Universitaires de France, 1954.

Lindsay, R. B. "Entropy Consumption and Values in Physical Science," *American Scientist*, XLVII (1959), 376-385.

Locke, John. *An Essay Concerning Human Understanding*, ed. A. C. Fraser, 2 vols. New York: Dover, 1959.

Łukasiewicz, Jan. *Aristotle's Syllogistic: From the Standpoint of Modern Formal Logic*. 2 ed. Oxford: Clarendon Press, 1957.

May, Rollo. "The Nature of Creativity," *Creativity and its Cultivation*. New York: Harper, 1959, pp. 55-68.

Poincaré, H. "Mathematical Creation" from *Science and Method* collected in *The Foundations of Science*. Lancaster, Pa.: The Science Press, 1946, pp. 383-394.

Ross, W. D. *Aristotle*. New York: Meridian, 1959.

Ross, W. D., ed. *The Works of Aristotle Translated into English*. 12 vols. London: Oxford University Press, 1928-1952, esp. vol. 1.

Schlegel, Friedrich von. *Kritische Schriften*, ed. W. Rasch. München: Hanser, 1938.

Schon, D. A. *Displacement of Concepts*. London: Tavislock, 1963.

Spinoza, Benedicti de. *Opera*, eds. J. van Vloten and J. P. N. Land. 2 vols. 3 ed. Hague: Nijhoff, 1914.

Whyte, L. L. *The Unconscious before Freud*. London: Tavislock, 1962.

Wiener, Norbert. *The Human Use of Human Beings*. 2 ed. Garden City: Doubleday Anchor Books, 1954.

Index